LADDER TO LEADERSHIP

LEADING ISN'T FAILING OTHERS

DEEPAK AGRAWAL

Revised Edition

BlueRose ONE.com
Stories Matter
NewDelhi • London

BLUEROSE PUBLISHERS
India | U.K.

For permissions requests or inquiries regarding this publication, please contact:

BLUEROSE PUBLISHERS
www.BlueRoseONE.com
info@bluerosepublishers.com
+91 8882 898 898
+4407342408967

ISBN: 978-93-5989-413-3

Cover Design: Sadhna
Typesetting: Pooja Sharma

First Edition: February 2024

BHAGAVAD GITA ||3.21||

"YADYADAACHARATI SHRESHTHASTATTADEVETARO JANAH;

SA YATPRAMAANAM KURUTE LOKASTADANUVARTATE"

यद्यदाचरति श्रेष्ठस्तत्तदेवेतरो जनः।
स यत्प्रमाणं कुरुते लोकस्तदनुवर्तते।। 3.21।।

WHATSOEVER A GREAT MAN DOES,

OTHER COMMONERS DO THE SAME;

WHATEVER STANDARD HE SETS UP,

THE WORLD FOLLOWS THAT.

Dedication

Dear Wife Manisha,

I want to express how important you were to me. The time we spent together were the happiest years of my life. You provided me with understanding, support, and love like no one else. You inspired me in ways I can't fully describe. You were always my biggest supporter, cheering me on the loudest. Whenever I was worried, you reassured me that things would be alright. When I was unsure of what to do, you always found a solution. When things got tough, you were a pillar of strength. Even during your illness, when I was at my wits' end, you held my hand and gave me hope that everything would be alright. I miss you!!

Dear Mom and Dad,

This book is dedicated to you for planting the seed of knowledge in my mind and lovingly nurturing it. I only realized later that you had instilled most of the leadership lessons in my mind through fables, anecdotes, and stories. Mom, I use your idioms during my meetings, and they are relevant and far more effective than the A-grade business school management courses.

Acknowledgment

The reason behind my decision to write and share my experiences comes down to gratitude— and a deep appreciation for the individuals who guided me on my journey and supported me along the way. I owe so much to them, as my life's trajectory wouldn't be the same without their influence.

My accomplishments owe a debt of gratitude to numerous mentors, each unique in their own way - young or old, junior or senior, male or female. Their advice and insights were invaluable and indispensable to my success. Beyond just guidance, having someone to lean on during tough times and opening doors to new opportunities has been truly meaningful. I've had the privilege of tapping into their wisdom and support, which has significantly contributed to my achievements. The weight of appreciation I carry for each and every one of them is immense.

The influence of a mentor is undeniably invaluable in propelling an individual toward their goals. It's worth noting that even iconic figures like Lord Rama and Krishna had mentors during their formative years.

Kindness possesses an extraordinary ability to improve the world - a principle I hold close to my heart. This is why I'm committed to paying forward, mirroring the help I've received. My aspiration is to translate my experiences into inspiration, motivating others to foster positive changes in their lives.

Furthermore, I'd like to take this moment to express my gratitude and love for the team behind this project and for my life as a whole. First, I'd like to thank my two kids, **Harsh Agarwal, my incredible Son, and Shikha Pandey, my immensely talented colleague,** for their unwavering belief in me! My writing life would not be possible without your support in helping me find my voice, a direction, a community, and a future.

I thank the many contributors essential to its final form: my team, Parthsarthi, Artists Swati, Sushmita Lakra, and Sadhna, for their fine artwork; Pooja for the Interior layout; and Rishabh and Simran for coordinating the work with me for publication. Their dedication and hard work have been instrumental in making this project a success. I'm deeply appreciative of their efforts.

I thank the writers, leaders, and teachers in my life for their support, encouragement, inspiration, ideas, sincerity, and dedication to their own craft. Thank you for your abundant supply of resources and information. This has helped me identify what is good about my work and make it even better. Much of my learning from such writers, scientists, and researchers is reflected in this book, too!

Foreword

Deepak Agrawal's book Ladder to Leadership: Leading Isn't Failing Others takes a giant step towards illuminating a very murky corner of our current world—leadership. Crying for authentic and effective leadership, we need this corner to be illuminated and made accessible so we can develop the leader within each one of us. Leadership is a field where we admire examples and get nuggets of wisdom from those who are accomplished. But discussing the same is always almost anecdotal, with tips and techniques that might sound like an interesting story. However, we are always left with this question: What do I do? Leadership is a performance art; instead of only concepts, it must be a field of actions, skills, and tangible results. The author's approach provides exactly the needed perspective. He reveals key actions, skills, and ways to make them work that are essential for an effective leader, manager, professional, or anyone who creates a future with others—and that includes all of us. Unlike other business books, Ladder to Leadership incorporates concepts from quantum mechanics and neuroscience to offer a unique perspective. The lessons in this book come from Deepak Agrawal's many years of supporting leaders and leadership teams as they overcome the common and recurring blind spots of leadership. He walks the talk because his results are the results of others. I have had the privilege of watching his leadership journey and working under his guidance for 11 years until now, observing him as he faces all the challenges of leadership, experiences both successes and failures, confronts himself, and actively engages in the path of practice to continuously learn and grow. Through his continued exploration, he has forged his own path. Sharing one's knowledge is a great way to build a brand, and through his book, he leads a pathway as to how we must engage to be effective in our leadership journey. This is an easy book to read. You can flip to any page and land on a compelling leadership lesson. Read a chapter, mull over the advice, let it marinate, put it into practice, and move on to savor another. Enjoy your exploration with Deepak Agrawal, and may it be one step of many in your leadership journey.

Priyaraj Beura

Lead Business & Sales Analyst

Jindal Stainless Ltd

Contents

Introduction

At its core, this book presents a captivating diary in an attempt to address pesky, frequently asked questions about leadership. Its ultimate purpose is to engage in a conversation, drawing from my 35 years of experience and multiple encounters with C-suite executives. Through my journey, I have realized that no scripted document on leadership can provide a comprehensive understanding of the complex interplay between People, Success, and Values. The concept of success goes beyond mere goal setting and the relentless pursuit of accomplishments; it extends beyond polished news releases or conclusive annual reports. Instead, it unveils a profound narrative centered around the art of problem-solving, as success is not a fixed destination but an ongoing journey that never ceases. Along this path, each triumph gives rise to new challenges, embodying the true essence of continuous growth and achievement.

But before delving into the diary of understanding great leaders, it would be beneficial to commence exploration with the opening segment, **Part I** of the book. This section serves as a foundation for gaining a more perceptive comprehension of the fundamental importance of leadership. Within these pages, the concept of leadership is thoroughly dissected and examined from various perspectives, encompassing its historical origins to its contemporary interpretations.

Outstanding leadership is crucial to the success of any organization. I believe that there is a set of skills that increases a leader's effectiveness in creating high-performing organizations, which helps them maintain resilience in the face of stress. These skills develop a leader's ability to stay connected to their source of meaning and purpose and to activate this connection in others. However, there is no blueprint available for what outstanding leadership looks like. Still, we will delve into the psychology and attributes of some of the most outstanding leaders available for our reference, both from the past and the present, along with their spiritual teachings and learnings in the **"Three Chapters of Part II."**

Chapter#1

In the realm of Quantum Leadership, we aim to understand the harmonious integration of leadership and spiritual intelligence. This section examines how a leader's spiritual quotient can be effectively integrated into their leadership style, providing valuable insights that extend beyond traditional leadership theory. Should you choose to seek the enlightened counsel of the revered Gurus, you shall unlock the transformative power to perceive untapped possibilities and fortuitous opportunities that elude the grasp of others.

Chapter#2

In this Chapter, we have the opportunity to explore leadership diversity with the Paragons, a group of exceptional leaders who possess distinct approaches and traits. These extraordinary qualities defy conventional norms and offer a refreshing perspective on effective leadership. By exploring their transformative insights, you will uncover a valuable set of toolkits to tackle and overcome leadership challenges, ultimately leading to a reduction in burnout.

Chapter#3

The concept of Leadership Reimagined is rooted in a thorough understanding of spiritual intelligence and the characteristics of non-traditional leaders, as explored in the initial chapters. This idea can potentially generate a more impactful fusion within the realm of leadership. The intention here is to use strategic leverage and thoughtful implementation of acquired knowledge to achieve favorable outcomes.

Finally, **Part III** is a journey into the world of myth and legacy with the Leaders of Mythology. This section sheds light on timeless narratives to illuminate some crucial leadership principles. By connecting mythological stories to modern leadership challenges, we can gain a deeper appreciation for the universal truths that underpin effective leadership.

As you navigate through the contents of this book, you will discover a captivating blend of three I's, i.e., **Insights, Ideas, and Inspiration**.

I sincerely hope this book provides something valuable for all of you, whether you are a budding leader aspiring to grasp the fundamentals, an accomplished leader pursuing novel insights, or just a curious individual intrigued by the art of leadership. Brace yourself for a transformative odyssey to enrich our understanding of leadership and illuminate a path toward heightened impact and influence.

As they say in -The Katha Upanishad[1]

"You are what your deep driving desire is

As is your desire, so is your will

As is your will, so is your act

As is your act, so is your destiny."

So, the key lies in embracing our true purpose and values, as they serve as the gateway to unlocking our future accomplishments and fulfilling our aspirations.

[1] **The Katha Upanishad** (Sanskrit: कठोपनिषद्) (Kaṭhopaniṣad) is an ancient Hindu text and one of the *mukhya* (primary) Upanishads, embedded in the last eight short sections of the *Kaṭha* school of the Krishna Yajurveda. It is also known as the *Kāṭhaka* Upanishad and is listed as number 3 in the Muktika canon of 108 Upanishads.

PART-I

Perspectives of Leadership

The concept of leadership is like a multifaceted diamond, reflecting different dimensions when viewed from various angles. These perspectives enrich our understanding of how leadership operates and its intangible impact on individuals, groups, and societies. From a psychological standpoint, leadership is an exploration of how individuals influence and guide others, often rooted in traits, behaviors, and situational dynamics.

Sociologically, leadership is the intricate interplay between leaders and followers, shaping norms, values, and collective goals. Whereas, within organizations, leadership acts as the cement that holds different elements together to form a foundation for achieving objectives through strategic vision, team coordination, and fostering an environment that promotes growth and development.

Each viewpoint offers a different lens, illuminating the many facets that comprise leadership. Organizational theory sheds light on the critical function of leadership in driving forward growth, while psychology and sociology delve deeply into the complexity of human relationships.

Through the integration of these perspectives, we can develop a comprehensive understanding of leadership that transcends its superficial portrayal. The convergence of these diverse viewpoints enables us to approach leadership with depth, adaptability, and a keen awareness of its transformative potential.

- ## Leadership in Academia— What is it?

Leadership, as a concept, has traversed time, cultures, and contexts, shaping the way individuals and groups function, progress, and thrive. Academically, it's not just a buzzword but a field of study that seeks to uncover the nuance of effective guidance and influence. Scholars have dissected the roots of leadership, tracing its evolution from ancient civilizations to the modern-day corporate world.

Historically, leadership was often viewed as synonymous with power and control. Rulers, kings, and monarchs exemplified leadership through authority and dominance. However, contemporary academic examinations have broadened this perspective. Leadership isn't confined to positions of authority; it thrives in various forms and at multiple levels within organizations, communities, and societies.

Scholars explore various theories to shed light on the mechanisms that underpin effective leadership. From Trait Theory, which focuses on the inherent qualities of leaders, to Situational Leadership Theory, which emphasizes adapting leadership styles to fit specific situations, these theories provide frameworks for understanding the complex interplay between leaders, followers, and environments.

Furthermore, academic inquiry into leadership encompasses a range of leadership styles. Leadership isn't a singular approach; it encompasses a spectrum of styles that leaders adopt based on their personalities, organizational culture, and goals. Some leaders opt for a democratic style, involving team members in decision-making processes. In contrast, others might adopt a transformational approach, inspiring followers to transcend their own interests for the collective good.

Academic discourse around leadership doesn't rely on a one-size-fits-all definition. Instead, it acknowledges the dynamic nature of leadership and the diverse contexts in which it operates. This perspective recognizes that leadership isn't limited to hierarchical structures; it can manifest as influence, guidance, vision, and empowerment.

Academic exploration doesn't stop at dissecting the leadership process; it extends to understanding its impact. Effective leadership has been linked to improved team dynamics, higher productivity, and enhanced organizational outcomes. Scholars scrutinize the ripple effects of leadership, studying how leaders shape organizational culture, drive innovation, and foster employee engagement. It appreciates that leadership adapts to contexts, embracing a multitude of styles and approaches.

This exploration bridges the gap between theoretical constructions and real-world applications, offering insights that resonate far beyond the confines of textbooks. Ultimately, an academic understanding of leadership equips individuals with the knowledge and perspectives to become more impactful leaders, capable of navigating the multifaceted challenges of today's dynamic world.

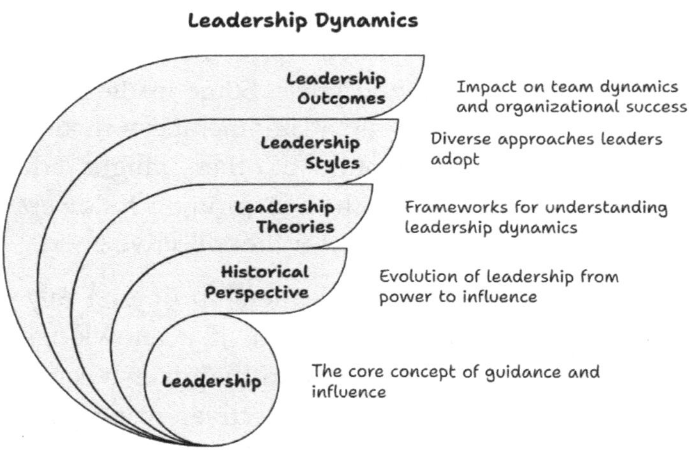

- ## A Brief Overview of Leadership Styles— A Scientific Perspective

Imagine leadership traits as the building blocks that construct the essence of a leader. This notion prompted Thomas Carlyle to propose the Great Man Theory in 1840. However, not everyone agreed. Two decades later, Herbert Spencer[i] argued against Carlyle's idea. He believed that leadership qualities weren't hardwired into specific individuals but rather developed over time through learning and life experiences. Spencer championed the Organic Theory, suggesting that leaders emerge organically from the collective awareness of a society.

Taking a broader view that encompasses external influences, Georg W. Allport[ii], spanning the years from 1897 to 1967, categorized a staggering 4500 mental, physical, and social characteristics into a hierarchical structure of three levels. From this concept, the Trait Theory emerged, aiming to isolate the distinctive attributes that define leaders. However, despite its endeavors, this theory couldn't pinpoint a definite set of qualities that universally define leaders.

Enter the Behavioral Theory, [iii] which offers a fresh perspective by shifting the focus from personal traits to actions. For instance, McGregor in 1960 and Blake and Mouton in 1964 emphasized what leaders do rather than who they inherently are. These theories introduced the notion that leadership can be cultivated through training, rather than being inherited.

Fiedler [iv], in 1964, steered the conversation toward Contingency Theories[v], suggesting that there is no one-size-fits-all leadership style. He proposed that the most effective style depends on the specific situation at hand. Hersey and Blanchard, in 1969, further developed this idea with their Situational Theory[vi], advocating for adaptability on the part of the leader.

John Adair[vii], in 1973, offered a more holistic approach, asserting that a leader must strike a balance between meeting 'task,' 'team,' and 'individual' needs. In 1978, MacGregor Burns[viii] introduced a moral and motivational dimension to leadership. He coined the term

Transformational Leadership [ix], highlighting leaders' capacity to inspire and empower their followers, guiding them to become not just followers but moral agents.

Charismatic Leadership[x], initially introduced by Weber in 1947 and later expanded upon by House in 1976, merged aspects of the Transformational Theory with earlier 'Trait' and 'Great Man' Theories. This style gained significant traction in the 1980s and 90s, portraying charismatic leaders as visionaries who offer inspiration during economic downturns. Yet, the 21st century brought corporate scandals that cast doubt on its effectiveness.

This led to a shift towards a more ethical dimension of leadership, as exemplified by the emergence of Servant Leadership [xi] (Greenleaf, [xii] 1970). This concept views leaders as facilitators, nurturing the growth and well-being of their teams and organizations, emphasizing humility, empathy, and the greater good over individual ambition.

Finally, Gronn introduced the concept of Distributed Leadership in 2002, breaking free from the confines of traditional organizational hierarchies. This perspective suggests that leadership influence isn't solely tied to roles and positions; individuals at all levels can exert leadership impact.

The scientific exploration of these various styles enriches our understanding of what it truly takes to lead effectively. This deeper comprehension empowers us to navigate the dynamic challenges of leadership roles with adaptability, empathy, and an invincible commitment to the betterment of individuals, teams, and organizations. Just as we probe the depths of quantum mechanics to unravel its mysteries, we continue to unravel the complexities of leadership, enhancing our ability to lead with purpose and impact.

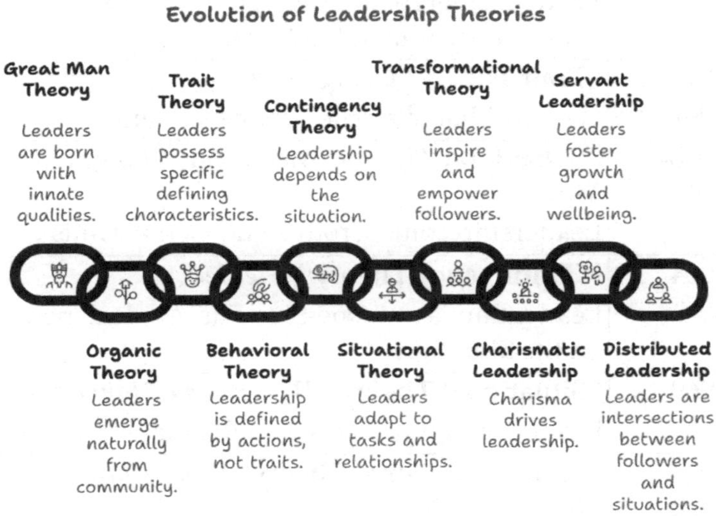

Leadership: A Historical Overview	
1840	**"Great Man Theory"** ***Thomas Carlyle*** Leaders are innately Hardwired
1860	**"Organic Theory"** ***Herbert Spencer*** Leaders emerge naturally from shared Community understandings.
1897-1967	**"Trait Theory"** ***Georg W. Allport*** Certain Characteristics define leaders
1960-1964	**"Behavioral Theory"** ***McGregor, Blake, and Mouton*** Leadership comes from Actions, not Traits
1964	**"Contingency Theory"*****, Fiedler*** Leadership is not One-Size-Fits-All; It depends on the Situation
1969	**"Situational Theory"** ***Hersey and Blanchard*** Leaders adapt to Tasks and Relationships
1973-1978	**"Transformational Theory"** ***John Adair and MacGregor Burns*** Leaders are defined by their capacity to Inspire and Empower followers
1947-1976	**"Charismatic Leadership Theory"** ***Weber and House*** Charisma drives leadership, A combination of "Great Man" and "Traits"
1970	**"Servant Leadership"** ***Greenleaf*** Leaders foster Growth and Wellbeing
2002	**"Distributed Leadership"** ***Gronn*** Leaders are the intersection between Followers and Situations

- **Modern Perspective on Leadership— Beyond IQ and EQ**

Traditional metrics, such as IQ and EQ, have become inadequate for evaluating leaders in today's complex society. There's no denying the difficulty and pressure that comes with being in a leadership position. Although a high Physical Quotient (PQ) has always been crucial for leaders, the Spiritual Quotient (SQ) is a relatively new factor that is becoming increasingly significant.

It's essential to set the record straight that spirituality, in this sense, has nothing to do with religious piety, worship, or holiness. Instead, it emphasizes seeking more profound significance in life and realizing that there's more to us than just eating and sleeping. It takes into account the broader picture of our responsibilities as global citizens and as leaders who recognize the importance of reducing our environmental impact.

As our society has transitioned from a "Need and Greed" mindset to a "Wealth and Wisdom" mindset, the relentless pursuit of material possessions, often fueled by greed, has been replaced by a more enlightened perspective that values living in harmony with the environment and promoting the well-being of individuals.

Our perception of wealth has evolved, as we now acknowledge that it encompasses more than mere monetary assets. However, it is vital to avoid harboring an insatiable desire for money while still acknowledging its value.

Greed is a bottomless pit, whereas money itself is not inherently evil; it is the excessive longing for money that causes trouble. It is wise to accumulate wealth before embracing a spiritual life; however, personal gain should not take precedence over the betterment of society in the pursuit of wealth. Even the renowned great Buddha was once a prince. We can truly give to others or forego only when we have abundance.

In short, the contemporary perspective on leadership emphasizes the interconnectedness of our deeds, the world, and our own growth. The sustenance of the Earth extends beyond materialism and reaches a deeper level. Much like Copenhagen's interpretation[2], which explores the inherent complexity of quantum mechanics, where an object exists simultaneously in several distinct states until a conscious observer observes it, our understanding of leadership is also constantly evolving. It encourages us to seek knowledge and equilibrium, highlighting that leadership requires more than just knowledge and emotions.

SQ surpasses conventional attributes, such as intelligence and social skills. It hinges on creativity, the art of questioning, and the ability to see things holistically. It prompts us to view ourselves and our endeavors within a global, environmental, and human context. High SQ entails looking beyond the traditional role of enterprises as mere value-generating machines. It acknowledges their social and cultural responsibilities—the crux of SQ lies in the quest for a deeper life purpose.

[2] The **Copenhagen interpretation** is a collection of views about the meaning of **quantum mechanics**, stemming from the work of Niels Bohr, Werner Heisenberg, Max Born, and others. The term "Copenhagen interpretation" was apparently coined by Heisenberg during the 1950s to refer to ideas developed between 1925 and 1927, glossing over his disagreements with Bohr.

Our unique ideals and aspirations shine through the fabric of life and illuminate our path to fulfillment. These cornerstones of our existence go beyond simple aspiration; they embody the very core of who we are and what we aim to accomplish. We meet the winners who, despite the diminishing returns, refuse to give up their habit of winning.

Practicing patience, tenacity, and other virtues is always a great opportunity. After all, the trip itself, rather than the final destination, is what determines our fate.

With our principles as a rock and our aspirations as fuel, we embrace the spirit of evolution as we traverse the treacherous terrain of life. Like a rock that evolves into the moon, we too undergo a metamorphosis that ultimately benefits ourselves and everyone we encounter.

With the progress of society, it is evident that there has been a significant change in perspective globally. It is now acknowledged that the happiness index is equally, if not more important, than relying solely on GDP as a measure of success. Even the world's most robust economies are falling behind in this regard; however, fortunately, the concept of going beyond GDP has gained traction in recent years.

"GDP doesn't add up without well-being and happiness."

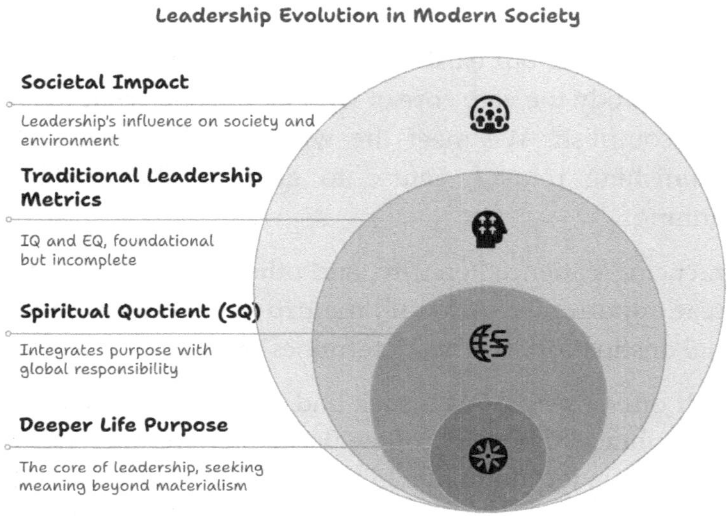

Several visionary thinkers are already revolutionizing the business landscape with their progressive ideas:

- Brian Bacon[3] of the Oxford Leadership[xiii] Academy redefines management consulting by emphasizing authentic leadership, genuine corporate social responsibility, and pragmatic spirituality.

[3] **Brian Bacon** and IPC (1983–2005) The founder of Oxford Leadership Academy (OLA), Brian Bacon, first started working with leadership in 1983 when he formed the management consulting branch of the global advertising agency DDB Needham. Through a buyout in 1990, the branch separated from DDB Needham and became International Pacific Consulting (IPC), which would later be renamed Oxford Leadership Academy. IPC worked with several major companies, including McDonald's, over the following years. Charlie Bell, who was the CEO of McDonald's in 2003, contacted Bacon and his company due to a massive decline in the stock market value, from $42 to $11. Brian Bacon and his team worked to revitalize the public image of McDonald's, resulting in a greater emphasis on the company's environmental initiatives, as well as modifications to its products and supply chain. The McDonald's stock started to recover and doubled in value over 6 months, although this success cannot be solely attributed to IPC.

- Chade-Meng Tan [4], a Google Fellow, advocates mindfulness through meditation, aiming to cultivate effective and innovative leaders using scientifically-backed mindfulness training while striving for global harmony.
- Jürgen Appelo [5], a leading management thinker challenges conventional thinking with creative management approaches, aiming to break free from entrenched traditional molds.

Significantly, a broad spectrum of organizations, ranging from governments to businesses, are not merely acknowledging the wisdom of these trailblazing thinkers and influencers; they are also translating their insights into tangible, actionable steps. Because in the world of business, people are the heartbeat behind success or failure. Beyond numbers, it's the quality of individuals that genuinely matters. Success hinges on the contributions of talented and effective people, while failure often results from the inadequacy of key team members. Business isn't just about

[4] **Chade-Meng Tan** (Chinese: 陳一鳴), known informally as Meng, is an author, philanthropist, motivator, and former software engineer. He was previously employed at Google, where he greeted celebrities who visited the Google campus. He retired from Google as its "Jolly Good Fellow" at the age of 45. He co-founded the Search Inside Yourself Leadership Institute, along with Marc Lesser, and serves as co-chair of One Billion Acts of Peace, which has been nominated for the Nobel Peace Prize eight times. He is also an adjunct professor at the Lee Kuan Yew School of Public Policy in Singapore, and he holds a degree from Nanyang Technological University.

[5] **Jurgen** is a versatile individual who identifies himself as a creative networker. He has been recognized as a top leadership expert and speaker by Inc.com. Since 2008, Jurgen has maintained a popular blog on NOOP.NL, where he shares ideas on agile management and organizational change. He has also authored several successful books, including Management 3.0, How to Change the World, Managing for Happiness, and Startup, Scaleup, Screwup. In addition to his professional pursuits, Jurgen is currently working on a science fiction novel titled Glitches of Gods.

figures; it's about the individuals who drive innovation, customer satisfaction, and progress. The secret of triumph lies in the excellence of the team as they shape the narrative of prosperity. Conversely, failure often stems from the inefficiency of those entrusted with critical roles. Successful businesses are built on people.

Today's leaders need a broader set of competencies to succeed in the modern world. It requires combining emotional intelligence with physical vigor and a strong sense of purpose to create a leader with all three qualities. This modern viewpoint acknowledges that leadership is more than just guiding businesses; it also includes the need to shape a future that aligns with broader societal and ethical concerns.

As we navigate this moment of radical change, leaders equipped with these nuanced understandings will be best positioned to steer their businesses toward a future that prioritizes purpose and sustainability over mere growth, progress, or development.

So, what is the typical difference between growth, development/progress, and success? Let's understand that the concept of **growth** frequently revolves around materialistic pursuits. We tend to measure progress by the accumulation of possessions and wealth. However, genuine **progress**—the kind that truly moves us forward as a society—is achieved when we prioritize ethical values and principles in our pursuits.

But **success**, the ultimate achievement, goes even further. It encompasses not only material gains and ethical behavior but also the qualities that make us distinctly human - our empathy, our sense of right and wrong, and our spiritual connection. When we harmonize all these elements in our lives, we achieve an ethereal state of success that goes beyond superficial measures. It's a kind of success that enriches not only our own lives but also the lives of those around us, contributing positively to our shared human experience.

Growth	=	*Accumulation of Material and Wealth*
Progress	=	***Growth*** + *Ethical Behaviour or Conscience*
Success	=	***Progress*** + *Empathy, Spirituality, or Humanity*

PART-II

CHAPTER-1

Quantum Leadership: The Basics

• Context of Theory and Leadership

Quantum leadership is an innovative management approach that combines effective traditional leadership practices with recent breakthroughs in quantum physics and neuroscience. A quantum leader is someone who recognizes their role as a co-creator of reality and actively influences it through their thoughts, beliefs, and goals. By shaping and transforming their visions into tangible outcomes, they can bring about meaningful change and innovation. Neuroscience research has shed light on how the brain's ability to adapt and change, known as neuroplasticity [6], can be harnessed through specific techniques. Likewise, certain principles of quantum physics suggest that reality can be altered through conscious observation. By cultivating a state of heightened

[6] **Neuroplasticity**, also known as **neural plasticity** or **brain plasticity**, is the ability of neural networks in the brain to change through growth and reorganization. A rewired brain behaves differently than it did before. These changes range from the formation of new connections within individual neuron pathways to systematic adjustments, such as cortical remapping or neural oscillations. Other forms of neuroplasticity include homologous area adaptation, cross-modal reassignment, map expansion, and compensatory masquerade. A new ability, information acquisition, environmental influences, practice, and psychological stress are examples of neuroplasticity. Neuroplasticity was once thought by neuroscientists to manifest only during childhood, but research in the latter half of the 20th century showed that many aspects of the brain can be altered (or are "plastic") even through adulthood. However, the developing brain exhibits a higher degree of plasticity than the adult brain. Activity-dependent plasticity can have significant implications for healthy development, learning, memory, and recovery from brain damage.

awareness and utilizing meditation practices, leaders and managers can refine their thought patterns to achieve desired goals, foster creativity, and enhance overall performance.

The science behind the various phenomena outlined above is still emerging. The evidence increasingly points towards a recurring theme: the power of your beliefs and convictions greatly influences your potential for creating a better future.

So, what do Quantum mechanics, Neuroscience, and Spirituality have to do with great leadership ability?

Lots, if you consider this question: What if business leaders, political leaders, or even self-leaders, for that matter, could tap into some of the mental energy harnessed by the Shaolin monks[7]?

Before proceeding further, let's consider the relationship between neuroscience and spirituality in the context of leadership. For most people, someone in a position of authority is automatically perceived as a leader. In consequence, leadership is viewed as a way of getting people to do what the 'leader' wants, often through their powerful position. Yes, it is true that a leader must convince others to follow them, but is that the primary purpose of leadership?

---

[7] **Shaolin Monastery** (少林寺; *shǎolínsì*), also known as Shaolin Temple, is a renowned monastic institution recognized as the birthplace of Chan Buddhism and the cradle of Shaolin Kung Fu. The town is located in Dengfeng County, Henan Province, China, at the foot of Wuru Peak. Besides its historical, cultural, and artistic heritage, the temple is famous for its martial arts tradition. **Shaolin monks** are devoted to research, creation, and the continuous development and perfecting of Shaolin Kung Fu.

If not, then what is authentic leadership after all?

The greatest leaders share two key characteristics: a burning desire to create a better future and perseverance in the face of formidable opposition. Rather than their authority, these two elements attract willing followers.

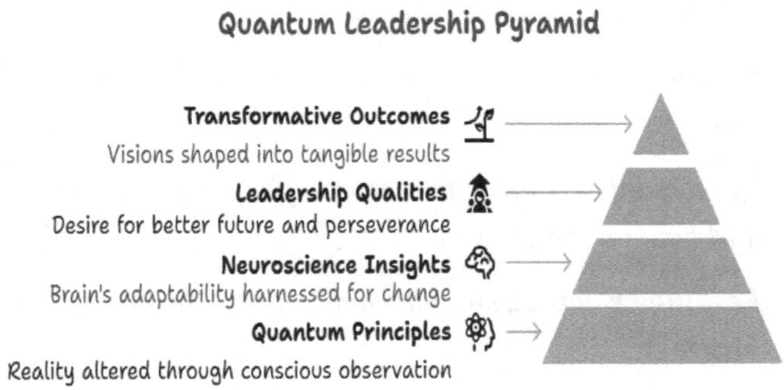

To continue to lead, the real question is: What energy sources enable true leaders to persist?

Based on my personal experience and experience observing good and bad leaders around the world spanning more than three decades, I believe leadership energy consists of three components:

- ✓ **Purpose**: The better future you want to create.
- ✓ **Values**: The principle of never compromising virtues under any circumstances.
- ✓ **Mindfulness**: Never stop living a life of values and purpose by harnessing the power of the mind.

Leadership Myths and Reality

- ✓ *Leadership is less about position, personality, competence, or heredity and more about choosing to strive hard to create a better future.*
- ✓ *The road to a better future is often paved with resistance—Leadership is often a thankless, lonely, and busy job without assurances of success.*
- ✓ *Non-leaders give up in the face of such resistance and low odds of success.*
- ✓ *Leaders must find leadership energy to overcome resistance and stay on the course.*
- ✓ *Leading is harnessing human energy to create a better future.*
- ✓ *Leadership energy is derived primarily from "clarity of purpose" and "clarity of values."*
- ✓ *Leaders who regularly still and calm their minds are more likely to be able to use their minds to influence reality.*

• Leadership, Gurus, and Spiritual Quotient (SQ)

Today's leaders must understand and accommodate a diverse range of people with different cultural, religious, and historical backgrounds, all while navigating the complex intersection of these factors. The concept of shared cultural values becomes even more complicated in a society where the pursuit of pleasure is a common goal. To be an effective leader in this context, we must prioritize the interests of our constituents above our own interests.

Thomas Friedman's perceptive insights from his immensely popular literary masterpiece, "The World is Flat," remain remarkably relevant in light of contemporary challenges such as global warming, ecological balance, the contamination of our precious air and water resources, deforestation, concerns regarding the fate of human civilization, and the shrinking amount of arable land per person. Friedman understood presciently how today's interconnected world enables people in different parts of the world to collaborate and compete in real-time, erasing distance barriers and creating a level playing field. The modern leader has both advantages and disadvantages in this ever-changing world.

Amidst the surge of interest in leadership studies within the academic realm, which has grown significantly in recent decades, there's a tendency to lean towards contemporary ideals like competition, individual growth, and self-fulfillment. However, it's essential to recognize the potential of contrasting traditional values, such as humility, gratitude, and community service, as an alternative approach.

When delving into the qualities and behavior patterns of leaders, specific attributes emerge as fundament:

- **Righteousness**: A leader's actions are guided by moral principles, fairness, and a sense of justice! They champion integrity within their realm, embodying the ethical values they advocate for. Without moral values and respect for the law and order, one can easily turn to a life of crime. Success at any price is hellish folly!
- **Protective, Caring, and Fair:** Leaders ensure the well-being and equity of their subordinates by creating an

environment of trust and respect. A genuine concern for the welfare of those they lead is a hallmark of effective leadership.

- And with a **Sense of Purpose**: Leaders can come to a better appreciation of who they are and what they want.

However, transcending the prosaic virtues, an exceptional leadership style is revealed through behavior patterns that extend beyond what meets the eye. Such leaders exhibit kindness and compassion in their guidance, making decisions rooted in fairness and justice and demonstrating the courage to stand up for their convictions. They don't just preach values; they live by them. They lead by example, even outside their comfort zone. By serving as role models through their conduct and attitude, they inspire not only their current followers but also future generations.

Authentic leaders, devoid of ego and power hunger, assume leadership roles because they are best suited for the responsibility. They serve as the heads of the joint family, responsible for fostering happiness among both employees and customers, and safeguarding the overall interests of the family as a whole. Their subordinates recognize their capability, trustworthiness, and suitability for the job. This mutual respect forms the bedrock of their leadership journey.

Integrity stands as the cornerstone of genuine leadership. True leaders uphold their values even in the face of adversity. Their actions consistently align with their beliefs, making them not just effective but also morally upright leaders.

Foundations of Effective Leadership

Cultural Understanding

Leaders must navigate diverse cultural backgrounds with empathy and respect.

Global Awareness

Leaders need to address global challenges like climate change and resource scarcity.

Traditional Values

Leaders should balance modern ideals with traditional virtues like humility and service.

Righteousness

Leaders must act with integrity and moral principles.

Protective Care

Leaders must ensure the well-being and fairness of their subordinates.

Sense of Purpose

Leaders need a clear understanding of their identity and goals.

Furthermore, a vital element in this paradigm is the mutual respect shared between leaders and subordinates. This respect forms the foundation of a healthy and productive working relationship, fostering collaboration, open communication, and shared success. Their leadership is exemplified by modesty, candor, and an expansive worldview that recognizes our shared humanity. "**When your mind is myopic, you never grow**!"

Unless you are clear about your purpose and your values and doing something that you really care about, it can be challenging to act as a leader. Within each of us resides a unique purpose, a guiding North Star that directs us toward our goals. This purpose serves as the driving force behind our actions, decisions, and aspirations. It kindles a fervent commitment to our objectives, empowering us to surmount challenges and setbacks. Amidst the fog of uncertainty, it offers clarity, stoking our determination and resilience to reach greater summits. This deep-rooted sense of purpose not only defines leaders' personal and professional quests but also enriches our sense of fulfillment and well-being.

As the Dalai Lama wisely puts it, "*Your purpose determines your power,*" highlighting the transformative force that purpose wields in our lives.

- **Cultivation of Spiritual Quotient in Leadership**

So, picture this: leadership isn't just something you're born with. Nope, it's like this garden you can grow and nurture. Crazy? But it's true. We can cultivate leadership qualities like we water our plants. The entire spiritual teaching rests on the axiom that virtuous qualities can be cultivated and achieved through practice and mindfulness. And guess what? This whole idea of Spiritual Quotient (SQ) revolves around a super cool concept of putting importance on morality, somewhat contradicts the leadership practices we observe in the Real world".

But one can actually develop them over time and move closer by recognizing the interconnectedness of all life and reflecting on one's actions and intentions." It's like becoming a better version of self."

Now, consider Quantum Physics, which suggests that matter, to some extent, is the product of consciousness; hence, the physical world is influenced by consciousness to some degree. In simpler terms, our thoughts and awareness can have a profound impact on the world around us.

And lastly, the notion that having good intentions alone isn't always enough; you need practical methods or mechanisms to achieve your goals effectively. In other words, while good intentions are important, having a well-thought-out plan or strategy is equally crucial for success.

Here's the deal: by understanding how everything's connected, you can get closer to becoming a top-notch leader. It's like realizing that your actions and intentions have a ripple effect that extends throughout the universe. You start to see the bigger picture, and that's when the magic begins to happen. The path to this kind of growth is open to anyone who's up for it. And if you're already proficient in these skills, you can certainly help those who are still finding their way. The great leader isn't some all-knowing ruler; they're more like a guide and a catalyst. Their goal? To make themselves kind of dispensable by helping others become self-sufficient.

Now, this whole process screams humility. Yes, you heard that right. A significant part of being a great leader is recognizing that you're not the center of the universe. It's like being self-aware enough to realize that your job isn't to be the ultimate authority. It's about being a helper, a mentor, and giving others the tools to shine on their own, much like the role of a parent.

So, let's take a quick ride through history. Leaders have been figuring themselves out for ages. As time goes on, they've been focusing on some key things that totally resonate with the whole SQ vibe: self-awareness, much like Ashoka[8] The Great, the ancient Indian emperor. His self-awareness emerged after witnessing the devastation caused by his own conquests, leading to a transformative shift in his leadership towards compassion and non-violence. It's like the path to great leadership isn't about bossing people around; it's about understanding yourself, positively impacting others, and having a big heart.

Firstly, there exists a pervasive notion that leaders possess an innate, almost magical personality that predestines them for leadership. It's as though leadership is etched into their genetic code. However, let's embark on a deeper exploration of this concept by delving into four key aspects that lie at the core of leadership discourse:

- A genuine Resume can be seen as a collection of life's challenges and hardships that reflect the concept of

[8] **Ashoka** (died 238 BCE, India) was the last major emperor of the Mauryan dynasty of India. His vigorous patronage of Buddhism during his reign (c. 265-238 BCE; also given as c. 273-232 BCE) furthered the expansion of that religion throughout India. Following his successful but bloody conquest of the Kalinga country on the east coast, Ashoka renounced armed conquest and adopted a policy that he called "conquest by dharma" (conquering by principles of right living). To ensure widespread awareness of his teachings and work, Ashoka utilized inscriptions on rocks and pillars at suitable sites. These inscriptions—the rock edicts and pillar edicts (e.g., the lion capital of the pillar found at Sarnath, which has become India's national emblem)—were mainly dated in various years of his reign.

Karma yoga[9], as presented in the Bhagavad Gita[10]. In this philosophy, one's actions, including the trials and tribulations faced, are integral to their spiritual journey and growth. There is more to a Resume of life than achievements; it is also about the lessons learned through suffering and experiences, as well as character and spiritual development.

- There is this universal hunt for leader qualities and behaviors. It's like trying to figure out what sets leaders apart.
- Can these qualities be nurtured and cultivated? Just as you can nurture and grow an oak tree, can you also train yourself to become a leader?
- Then, there's this whole ethical and social side of things. Like, what's the impact of leadership on you and the people you lead?

The question now is, is this worth it or practical? The whole focus on morality and ethics may appear to be a lofty or unrealistic concept, particularly in the competitive and ruthless environment we frequently encounter in today's world. It may seem like we don't have time for such things,

---

[9] **Karma yoga** is one of the four spiritual paths in Hinduism, one based on the "yoga of action", the others being *Jnana yoga* (path of knowledge), *Rāja yoga* (path of meditation) & *Bhakti yoga* (path of loving devotion to a personal god).

[10] **The Bhagavad Gita** ("Song of God or Lord") is among the most important religious texts of Hinduism and easily the best known. It is commonly referred to as the Gita and was originally part of the great Indian epic, the Mahabharata. Its date of composition, therefore, is closely associated with that of the epic—c. 5th–3rd century BCE—not all scholars agree that the work was initially included in the Mahabharata text, and so date it later to c. 2nd century BCE. It has been quoted by writers, poets, scientists, theologians, and philosophers—among others—for centuries and is often the introductory text to Hinduism for a Western audience.

and all we're focused on is trying to succeed. But hold on to a second:

- First, being a leader isn't solely about reaching the top; it's more about staying there with our heads held high.
- Second, we all humans have the desire for four things that pretty much everyone wants. Wealth, fame, a long life, and a grand existence. It seems that these are universal cravings, regardless of one's background. Interestingly, these desires align with Abraham Maslow's [11] Theory of Human Motivation [12], often regarded as the pinnacle of human needs.

However, some might wonder how these remarkable aspirations can be accomplished and sustained. Understanding karma (actions), characteristics, behavior, cultivation, and ethical and social aspects can be challenging to grasp their complexities. To help in understanding this interconnectedness and how essential human qualities contribute to effective leadership and

---

[11] **Abraham Harold Maslow** (1908 -1970) was an American psychologist who developed Maslow's hierarchy of needs, a theory of psychological health that prioritizes fulfilling innate human needs in order, culminating in self-actualization. Maslow was a psychology professor at Brandeis University, Brooklyn College, New School for Social Research, and Columbia University. He emphasized the importance of focusing on the positive qualities in people, rather than treating them as a "bag of symptoms." A *Review of General Psychology* survey, published in 2002, ranked Maslow as the tenth most cited psychologist of the 20th century.

[12] **Maslow's hierarchy of needs** is an idea in psychology proposed in his 1943 paper "A Theory of Human Motivation," published in the journal Psychological Review. It categorizes human needs into different levels, starting with basic physiological needs and progressing to higher-level emotional and intellectual needs. The theory is applied in various fields, including education, healthcare, and sociology. It emphasizes the importance of individualism and prioritizing needs. Although often depicted as a pyramid, Maslow did not create this visual representation himself. The hierarchy of needs is widely utilized in research, management training, and higher education.

success, a concise, four-step overview is presented below, followed by more detailed explanations later in the book.

❖ ***Magic of 4 Cs: Curiosity, Confidence, Courage, and Consistency***

Curiosity is the dynamic spark within the mind that triggers questions, unlocking the door to creativity and innovation.

Historically, when an apple fell on someone's head, the typical response was "Ouch" or "Gosh." But one day, a visionary asked, "Why?" Why did the apple fall down instead of floating away like a cloud or a leaf? This curiosity ignited Newton's discovery of the law of gravity.

Confidence is the next step of creative curiosity!

Asking the right questions—like who, why, what, when, and where—unleashes the realm of possibilities, solutions, motivations, and ultimately, confidence. Harness the power of five magical words: "I CAN DO IT TOO!" Speak these words aloud to yourself and share them with your positive-thinking friends.

Courage stems from intelligence, hidden instincts, and a silent and secret institution within. It's the unwavering assurance that says, "You can count on me, no matter what challenges come my way." It's the absence of negativism, of fearing failure, embarrassment, hurt, falling, love, or loss. Instead, it's the fear of never trying, never having faith, and missing out on the potential for success. It's like self-belief; believe in yourself, and you're already on your way.

Consistency or perseverance are the keys, as the Bible verse says:

"No one having put his hand to the plow, and looking back, is fit for the kingdom of God" (Luke 9:62).

The lesson here is to remain focused and committed to the tasks at hand. We must not get distracted or sidetracked by temptations or distractions. It's so important to finish it up, wrap it up, and never pack it away. Make sure everything is checked, double-checked, and rechecked!

❖ **Moral virtue.**

It's like doing the right thing even when no one's watching.

Call it moral virtues, responsibility, or accountability; it adds up to integrity! And integrity leaves little room for fear, as we know we have done the right thing. Good leadership involves moral integrity, consistently doing what's right, genuinely caring for others, and finding a meaningful connection.

Once, Chanakya was working under an oil lamp when a Chinese traveller visited his house. Upon finishing his tasks, he politely extinguished the lamp and replaced it with another. Curiously, the traveller asked if this practice was customary in India. In response, Chanakya clarified that although it was not a typical Indian custom, the first lamp was for official work and paid for by the National Treasury. His switch was a gesture to avoid utilizing national resources during their personal conversation.

It implies that effective leadership isn't just about pursuing success or rewards without ethical consideration. Instead, it's like saying you can actively pursue your dreams while excelling as a compassionate and ethical leader, bringing order and practicality to your leadership style while addressing both your personal and ethical goals.

❖ **Generosity:**

Regarding generosity, have you ever wondered how sharing good things with others can go a long way?

Success may or may not imply material abundance, but it undeniably contributes to the accessibility of education, healthcare, and entrepreneurial opportunities. So, genuine success means we are able to provide an outlet for our creative expression in the creation and distribution of products, enabling us to experience the joy of giving. The pleasure of contributing to noble causes and institutions in this world of hunger and pain, much like the philanthropic efforts of Princess Diana.

Reflecting on the stories of Princess Diana, we see the importance of grace, compassion, and using one's platform for positive impact. Her life serves as a poignant reminder of the positive influence we can have when we leverage our position to make a difference in the lives of others.

Success does mean that you have become a generous person. Leaders who actively contribute to and support their community understand that their role extends beyond personal gain, instead involving the empowerment of those around them.

As long as you can afford to give, you will never feel poor; you will always feel rich!

❖ **Wisdom:**

Yes, it's like the golden ticket that gets us those treasures!

Wisdom is not knowledge; wise possibility thinkers don't go off with wild, wacky moves, ignoring reality. Before plunging in and exploring the realm of possibilities, it's crucial to recognize your position and assess the competition.

An executive at Ford Motor Company once told me we had been frustrated trying to strengthen our position in the luxury car market. We haven't succeeded in dislodging Mercedes. They've got their position set so firmly, it's rough." So, no matter what possibilities we are latching onto, like a salesperson, by understanding our current position, we can better navigate the path to our desired destination. Cricketers know the advantage of a good position after winning the toss and the privilege of choosing batting or bowling, considering the wicket conditions and the opponent team.

"What happens is not as important as how you react to what happens." Storming ahead at full speed because of your ego needs or own enthusiasm, and disregarding competition or harsh reality, can be disastrous. This reminds me of a story of a battleship I read somewhere.

A battleship was on exercise at sea in bad weather. The captain was on the bridge. It was foggy. Just after dark, the lookout spotted a light on the starboard side. The captain asked if it was steady or moving. The lookout replied that the light was steady, meaning they were on a direct collision course with that ship! The captain ordered the lookout signal to the other ship:

"Change course 20 degrees. We are on a collision course."

The signal came back, "Advisable for you to change course."

The captain signalled, "I am a captain. Change course 20 degrees."

"I am a Seaman- second class. You had better change course 20 degrees," came the reply.

The captain was furious. He replied, "I am a battleship. Change course!"

Back came the signal, "I am a lighthouse. Your call."

What a face-pollen moment!

Preparedness to adapt and alter our course according to the unsatisfied wants of human beings is the key to success. Much like a ship adjusting its sails to changing winds or obstructions, we too must be ready to pivot and embrace change as we progress towards our goals.

So, the big question remains: Are great leaders born or made? Well, people have been debating this for centuries. There's no one-size-fits-all answer. The approach and skills vary as leadership isn't just a cookie-cutter thing. It's like a blend of self-centered goals and altruistic purpose, benefiting everyone.

So, to wrap it all up, the notion that leadership evolves from the womb is truly intriguing. Leadership is akin to a continuous journey of growth and development. It's not merely about holding a position of authority; instead, it's a process of continuous learning and personal growth that also involves inspiring and nurturing others. At its core, leadership is about forging connections, not just within the team but also with broader objectives and aspirations. Just as life evolves from its very beginning, so does effective leadership, and this concept underscores the dynamic and transformative nature of leadership. So, whether you're naturally a leader or you're working on becoming one, remember there's no fixed formula. It's like a recipe you create with a dash of values, a sprinkle of empathy, and a whole lot of heart.

- **"The Twelvefold Hypothesis" Understanding and Inculcating SQ in Modern Leadership**

Let's dive deeper into the heart of humanity's spiritual philosophy! Have you ever wondered what it's all about? It revolves around the pursuit of the ultimate common good – happiness – and the path that leads us there. It sounds like a big deal. Well, it is, particularly when we begin integrating these spiritual teachings into the framework of contemporary leadership.

Here's the lowdown: Meditation and chanting are indeed beneficial spiritual practices, but it's worth noting that they are not the only techniques available. A vast pool of wisdom also exists that can shed light on the path to effective leadership. Consider this: many of these spiritual teaching centers are founded on universal themes such as doing good, being honest, and loving your neighbor as yourself. They stress the value of conserving resources and urge people to cut back on greedy consumption.

In addition, spirituality encourages a transition from narrowly focused, egocentric, and ethnocentric viewpoints to broader, more global geocentric ones. This shift enables leaders to develop a keen appreciation for the world's interdependence and a strong sense of accountability. This comprehensive strategy aims to enhance leaders by fostering their self-awareness, social compassion, and personal accountability.

Now, if we could take a moment to go back in time, there used to be these notions about these super-leaders, who almost seemed like legendary figures destined for greatness. However, you may be surprised to learn that the exceptional qualities, such as emotions and intelligence, that contribute to becoming an outstanding leader are not simply bestowed upon individuals by the universe. Instead, they are acquired and refined through learning and experience. It can be said that leaders are developed and molded rather than inherently born with these attributes.

However, there is a catch: in this entire social circus, what we call life, leadership emerges when someone steps up to serve the needs of others. It's like saying, "Hey, I'm here to guide you and make things better for everyone." It's not about being the ruler on a throne; rather, it's about being a servant with a purpose.

Now, this is where things become interesting! If today's leaders are responsible for guiding business transformation, businesses should not define how leaders act, influence, and create momentum in search of future growth. To lead business transformation, leaders must learn how to transform themselves to define the future growth of their businesses.

The spiritual context of leadership, moral conduct, and benevolence is a prerequisite and does not contradict the pursuit of rewards. Leadership is all about acting—putting your words into motion. And what are the qualities that make a leader great? Well, are they like the tools in a superhero's utility belt? No, they're designed for leadership tasks, like making things happen smoothly, but with a unique approach to harness the human mind. The inclusive approach further enhances their ability to leverage their position and time, resulting in significantly increased effectiveness.

- **Becoming a 10X Programmer**: This concept is often associated with software development and means striving to be exceptionally productive and efficient. It implies delivering ten times the value or output compared to an average programmer through skills, tools, and effective problem-solving. For leaders, it signifies the apt allocation of resources by exercising sound judgment.

- **Position of Leverage**: This term refers to finding a strategic advantage or a favorable position that allows you to achieve more with less effort. Just as money can be leveraged through investments, and relationships can be leveraged for collaboration and support, effective leaders seek positions of leverage to maximize their impact.
- **Management and Value of Time**: The idea that "you can't keep renting your time" highlights the importance of using your time wisely. Leaders often prioritize tasks, delegate responsibilities, and use their time efficiently to focus on high-impact activities. Measuring time hourly and understanding its value in monetary terms is a common approach to assessing the cost and efficiency of activities. It helps individuals make informed decisions about how to allocate their time and resources.

One minute for seven (7) billion people of the world population underlines the immense value of time collectively; seven (7) billion minutes mean millennia! It emphasizes that time is a finite and precious resource, and how we use it individually and collectively can have compound impacts over extended periods.

The **"twelvefold hypothesis"** discussed in subsequent pages could potentially serve as a valuable guide for leaders. However, it is essential to note that it encompasses not only the end goal but also the entire process leading up to it. This mission must align with the grand vision of making things awesome for everyone and the common good. And it's not just lip service; leaders must walk the talk. It's like every move they make should reflect that mission, that vision, and that commitment to making things better.

Everything that happens to us in life has some origin in our thoughts, our beliefs, our emotions, and our perceptions. This implies that our mental landscape has a direct and substantial influence on our external surroundings. Our outlook and the choices we make determine the outcomes of our lives. When individuals possess a mindset infused with optimism, hope, and anticipation of a positive outcome, they are more inclined to confront challenges head-on. Conversely, adopting a defeatist or pessimistic perspective may impede progress or hinder swift advancements.

The way we perceive and react to the environment not only influences our thoughts and emotions but also our decisions, our relationships, and our future. The likelihood of taking risks and attempting to achieve one's goals is significantly influenced by the individual's assessment of their own talents and values. However, a person who is plagued by self-doubt or limiting beliefs may unknowingly erect barriers to their own success.

To sum up, spirituality isn't some abstract idea. It's a gold mine of information that may help guide organizations and their leaders. It's about being nice people who never compromise who they are. It's like taking those timeless lessons and updating them with today's sensibilities, incorporating them into your personality and leadership style. Focusing on the larger good, on pleasure, and on a path that lights the way for everyone is what true leadership is all about.

I. Pasts Cannot Be Changed

Let's talk about something we all can relate to— The Past. You know that collection of memories that we've left behind. It's like a trail of footprints leading us to where we are today. But here's the kicker - we can't change it; once something is done, it's done, unalterable by regret or wishful thinking. Yup, it's like a movie that's already played out, and unlike a movie, you can't hit the rewind button on life.

Regardless of the outcome—whether a failure, success, or partial success—the cool part is that it's not a dead-end street. This perspective implores us to view life as a continual voyage, one that we possess the power to shape through the lessons gleaned from our past and the choices we make. It beckons us to embrace failure with unwavering courage, recognizing it as a fortuitous blessing or an opportunity to venture into new and exhilarating adventures rather than succumbing to defeat. By shedding our apprehensions, we can now welcome fresh perspectives and eagerly explore uncharted territories.

Think about it: every choice we've made, every step we've taken has brought us here. And sure, not all those steps might have been in the right direction. Let's be honest for a second: we can't play the blame game and point fingers at others or the past. "Why me?" is a common question when facing challenges, hardship, or rejection. It's natural to wonder why we find ourselves in a particular situation.

I happened to come across an article about Arthur Ashe, a great player of his time. In 1975, Arthur Ashe won

Wimbledon, unexpectedly defeating Jimmy Connors to become the first black player to win a Grand Slam. During one of Ashe's two heart surgeries in 1988, he received blood transfusions that led to the development of HIV. Many asked him why God chose him out of all the people when he had not done anything wrong. To this, Ashe's reply was, "All over the world, some million teenagers aspire to become tennis players. Maybe a hundred thousand of those millions reach some sort of proficiency. Fewer than a thousand play on circuits, and only about a hundred play Grand Slams. Finally, only two reach Wimbledon's final. When I was standing with the Wimbledon trophy in my hand, I never questioned God, "Why Me?" And now, what right do I have to ask God, "Why Me?"

Yet, paradoxically, we often fail to acknowledge our blessings fully. When something positive occurs, we promptly claim credit and attribute it to our own efforts or deservingness. So, self-indictment for the negative results might be painful at times, but instead of blaming external factors or circumstances, we must focus on self-reflection and personal responsibility. It's about acknowledging that we can learn from our experiences, whether good or bad, and take ownership of our actions. Essentially, it's about acknowledging, "I could have done better," and using that mindset to drive growth and improvement. Our future doesn't have to be a carbon copy of our past.

But why's it such a big deal to let go of the past? Well, imagine this: you're driving a car. And you're fixated on the rear-view mirror, focused on what's behind you. What's gonna happen? You'll crash into something ahead because you're not looking where you're going. That's how life is when you're too wrapped up in the shadow of the past. It's like trying to move forward while being stuck in reverse.

You see, some people let their past define them. They would say, 'Oh, I messed up before, so I'm gonna mess up again.' And guess what? It becomes a self-fulfilling prophecy. But here's how you can change the narrative: if you believe that your future can be different, you can make it so. By staying prepared and optimistic about what lies ahead, you can navigate the twists of fate with confidence and turn opportunities into reality. Blind luck also only favors a prepared mind that is proactively planning for the future.

Now, let's consider bringing this down to earth. If your past is a playground of happiness, that's wonderful! Please continue to do what makes you happy, explore new opportunities, and continue to grow. However, if you're not entirely satisfied with how things are unfolding, here's a helpful suggestion: take a moment to peek at your past. Yeah, embrace it, but don't let it hold you hostage. Remember, your past doesn't control your future; you do!

Here's another tip: History in the curriculum is not just about learning dates and events; it's about learning from the vicarious experiences of the past. We learn more by getting things wrong than by getting them right. Making countless mistakes and learning from them can only increase the accuracy rate. So, multiply your learning vicariously; learn from history and the people around you, including your parents, friends, and relatives—they've stories too. Take their wisdom and learn from their hits and misses. Moreover, consider what you've already learned from life and the advice your future self would give you.

You've gained insight into where you stumbled and where you soared; it's like stepping into the shoes of a wiser self and taking those steps toward a better tomorrow.

This is precisely why learning from your mistakes and venturing into new endeavors is a wise move. Failure, once you've faced it, loses its grip on your fears. The past remains unalterable; it's a done deal. But here's the beauty of it: you're wiser now. You've gained insight into where you've stumbled and where you've soared. Consider your choices as little arrows - they have the power to either pull you down or catapult you toward the stars.

So, here's the bottom line: embrace your past, but don't let it hold you back. While your past might be a story, and immutable. But your future? Your future is like clay waiting to be molded by your choices!

II. Opinions Don't Define Reality

In our world, opinions are like the wind - they come and go but don't define who we are. There's a quote by Marcus Aurelius, a major truth bomb: "Everything we hear is an opinion, not a fact. Everything we see is a perspective, not the truth."

People talk. It's just a part of life. They yap about everything under the sun, from your fashion choices to your career decisions. Sometimes, they're like a pack of wolves, looking to pounce on anything they think is different or threatening to their idea of normalcy. It's like this unending cycle where no matter what you do, they're ready to pick you apart.

The problem is that we often allow their opinions to penetrate our very being. We let their words slip beneath our armor as if they hold the blueprints of our identity. But the unvarnished and objective truth is that other people's opinions are just as significant as yesterday's news. Honestly, there's no need to cling to every utterance they make.

And their thoughts? Well, they don't have the power to define who you are. Amid the noise, as exemplified by the famous adage of the deaf frog in the bell and the Bumblebee's defiance of aerodynamic limitations with its unique body shape and wing size, it becomes evident that self-serving conclusions should be held to a higher standard. Instead of getting lost in the noise, it's crucial to maintain focus on the problem at hand, recognizing that extraordinary solutions can often emerge from seemingly improbable circumstances.

This is the real kicker, though: It stings when someone purposely aims to hurt you. It's like they're playing darts with your emotions. And trust me, we've all been there. It's tough not to let their words take hold of your thoughts. It's like trying to block out a thunderstorm with a flimsy umbrella.

Let's rewind a bit. Back in the day, kids used to form groups, right? They'd stick together and sometimes gang up on others. It's as if there's a primal need to feel better by making someone else feel worse. But let's get one thing straight: nobody's better than you. Your skin color, your beliefs, your job— none of that makes you any less impressive. Sometimes, when people can't do something themselves, they try to convince you that you can't do it either. But if you really want something, go after it, and don't let anything stop you.

Living by your values and playing the long-term game with like-minded individuals is paramount. Rise above the noise and negativity. Take the high road. Don't let their judgments and opinions become your poison. And that's how your superhero cape comes in. Remember, they don't know your battles, your journey, or the mountains you've climbed. It's like they're trying to judge a book by its cover without even flipping the pages. Their views are like dusty old books with no relevance to your unique life story. So, stay focused on your values and long-term goals, as this is where your true power lies.

Adopting a pessimistic outlook is the easy way out, but finding an optimistic contrarian is rare. Our personal narrative exemplifies the remarkable influence of this perspective. To illustrate, imagine a man's gut reaction when he sees a Father at the train station who looks to be ignoring his children. But there's more to this tale than meets the eye. The father's grief is hidden from plain sight; he recently lost his wife to cancer and is struggling with telling his children the devastating news. The shift from judgment to empathy happens quickly, like when you finally unlock a secret.

So, let's sum this up. Your self-worth? It's not on sale for approval. People's opinions? They're like shadows – they're there, but they can't touch your core. So, chin up! You're the author of your life, and critics and naysayers are just scribbling in the margin. Your story is bold, beautiful, and uniquely yours. So, don't let anyone else's thoughts dictate your narrative.

Indeed, we can be thankful for the Disney Company today because Walt Disney chose not to heed his critics and instead pressed forward toward his dreams. His undeterred persistence led to the creation of one of the most popular and successful entertainment companies in the world.

III. Everyone's Journey is Unique

Let's explore the awesomeness of individuality together with the quote of "Benjamin Franklin," an American intellectual of his time, "We must indeed all hang together, or most assuredly, we shall all hang separately." It's like a poetic way of saying that each of us is walking our own path, and that's the heart of it.

First and foremost, it is important to acknowledge that everyone's journey is like a fingerprint—uniquely their own. We're all wired differently, with our own dreams, ambitions, and quirks. If you're wondering about the events that have unfolded in our lives, it's important to note that these experiences have influenced us in various ways, both positively and negatively. And as for how we respond to life, well, that's like a thumbprint—distinct and personal!

But here's the wisdom: being different doesn't make you terrible. Life's journey isn't a straight highway for anyone. We all have our share of twists and turns, bumps and detours. And guess what? That's okay! You see, you'll never have the same adventure as someone else, and that's the beauty of it.

I have fond memories of my younger days when I used to be significantly influenced by the opinions of others regarding my life choices. Those pesky timelines like getting married at 25 and having two kids by 30? Societal expectations at a specific age made me doubt myself and feel frustrated.

But here's the magic: choosing to be your own priority is like stepping into the spotlight. Closing the door on the world's assumptions is liberating. And to be honest, competing against yourself is the ultimate challenge. I've got this story! My son was preparing for the engineering entrance exam. One day, when I went to pick him up after a coaching session, I noticed his name was at the top of the grade list on the noticeboard. Feeling elated, I asked, "Hey, you didn't tell me you aced the last exam!" And he hits me with this wisdom: "Dad, it's not that I did well; it's that others didn't do well."

But let's address the elephant in the room- why compare? It's like being on an emotional rollercoaster. Why hurt yourself by measuring your journey against someone else's path? Seriously, don't. Be your own hype squad and start focusing on becoming the best version of yourself. It's about letting go of the urge to compare yourself to others. It's neither helpful nor fair, and honestly, not even relevant. You have your own dream. You've got to protect it!

Would you be willing to exchange your life with someone else? Hold up, here's a reality check. Your journey? It's not their journey. Their story? It's not your story. Oh, and by the way, have you ever noticed how people's lives are like Instagram posts? You're seeing a filtered snapshot, not the entire story. They could be fighting battles you know nothing about. Don't let that comparison game steal your happiness! It's like trying to compare apples and oranges or pizza and chocolate. So, next time you catch yourself in the comparison trap, pause. Is it even reasonable to measure your life against someone else's highlight reel? Odds are, it's not. Embrace your path, your uniqueness, and your values as they are the driving forces behind your exceptional journey, one that can't be compared to anyone else's."

How about we conclude this by acknowledging that your journey is truly exceptional? It wouldn't be fair to compare it to anyone else's, just as it wouldn't be fair to compare Picasso to Van Gogh. So, stop the self-judgment and ditch the comparisons! We all experience self-doubt, insecurity, or fear of failure at times. "You don't deny it, but you also don't capitulate to it. You choose to embrace it."

IV. With Time, Things Get Better

Just as the forces of nature meticulously shape glass in a furnace, they also sculpt our lives with precision and purpose. There is a common thread in all our experiences, challenges, and triumphs: the belief in the transformative power of time. In times of adversity, this notion provides solace and serves as a guiding light during life's storms. It's an abstract understanding that, no matter how daunting the present may appear, the future holds the promise of brighter days. To paint a vivid and expansive portrait of these enduring truths, let's explore how this concept relates to resilience, acceptance, self-care, and finding purpose in life.

"Tough times never last, but tough people do." Challenges eventually yield to relief, and just as life is a classroom, it imparts wisdom and experience over time. These lessons equip us to confront problems with finesse, transforming us into adept problem-solvers with a deeper understanding of our choices and the confidence to navigate life's storms.

This process is a unique privilege that we possess—the ability to reframe our narrative, shed the weight of past errors, and carve a new path towards the boundless horizon of possibilities. As we embark on this transformative journey, we set attainable goals and, through actionable steps, methodically pave the way to fulfillment. This journey serves as a reminder that greatness is an ongoing process shaped by our resilience, growth, and unwavering commitment to the pursuit of excellence.

Now, let's zoom in on the canvas of contemporary existence. The world has witnessed a cascade of crises lately, ranging from global pandemics that reshape our realities to deeply personal tragedies that have shaken the very sense of our being. We find ourselves grappling with a whirlwind of change, economic uncertainties, political unrest, and the raw force of natural disasters. Each day presents its own trials and tribulations.

Amid this turmoil, the mind becomes a battleground where stress and anxiety collide, giving birth to a sense of helplessness. It's like sailing on tumultuous seas, each wave threatening to capsize our mental and emotional equilibrium, leaving us vulnerable to the debilitating influences of numbing inertia, explosive anger, and the acute agony of denial. Moreover, the depths of despair can plunge us into the abyss of depression and disarray, where hopelessness reigns supreme. Yet, amidst this tempestuous turmoil, there lies a glimmer of possibility - the potential for acceptance and the eventual resumption of our inner strength. The weight of personal sorrows, the unbearable grief of losing cherished individuals, the gradual decline of our health, the harsh realities of unemployment, or a myriad of other adversities can further compound the chaos.

The journey of life often takes unexpected turns, and at times, it may seem like we're moving backward. However, the key is to keep following the road because the destination isn't tied to a specific direction but rather lies at the end of the road itself.

Here's the revelation: within each of us resides the incredible superpower of resilience. This remarkable trait has the ability to transform adversity into a stepping stone for growth and development. Resilience is the art of skillfully navigating through change, loss, and trauma, emerging from these trials even more robust and wiser than before. It's akin to possessing a trusty compass that guides us through uncharted waters, offering a lifeline of hope and determination when we feel lost or uncertain along the way.

"Pain is inevitable, suffering is optional" is a powerful reminder that we can choose how we respond to life's challenges. However, it's crucial not to mistake resilience for a quick achievement. Resilience isn't about suppressing emotions or numbing ourselves to pain; instead, it's a gradual process of nurturing self and acclimating to the changed condition. It involves acknowledging our emotional responses to life's trials and tribulations and recognizing that each of us has a unique way of processing and coping with difficulties. In essence, resilience is the conscious and evolving practice of harnessing our inner strength to grow stronger in the face of adversity.

Consider resilience as a toolkit, one that equips us with the tools to brave the storm. It allows us to stand tall, even in the face of the fiercest gales. Resilience helps us to stay focused amidst chaos, embrace uncertainty with a steady heart, manage strong emotions with grace, and nurture healthier relationships, all while bolstering our self-esteem. It's about mastering the art of overcoming obstacles and finding our footing once again.

And what's more? Resilience doesn't discriminate against anyone based on age, background, or circumstances. It's an open invitation extended to every soul willing to embark on the transformative journey. So, how do we cultivate and nurture this resilience within us? Let's uncover the secrets.

Consider it as discovering a silver lining: As fate dealt me the tragic blow of losing my beloved wife to swine flu, my son offered a poignant perspective, expressing gratitude and remarking, "Thank God it wasn't you; you both were traveling together." This earnest moment tested the emotional and financial fortitude of our family, and the thought of his mother's potential trauma was overwhelming. However, recognizing that the situation could have been even more dire was the initial step towards resilience.

It's like standing at a crossroads where you consciously opt to face reality rather than bury your head in the sand. Avoiding challenges might provide a fleeting illusion of control, but it's akin to constructing a fragile house of cards destined to crumble.

In contrast, acknowledging loss and allowing ourselves to grieve are essential steps toward acceptance—the very bedrock upon which resilience is built. It's akin to understanding that while we can't control the weather, we can master the art of sailing through life's tempests. In this analogy, the pilot symbolizes our agency and determination, guiding the course of the plane even when buffeted by unpredictable winds.

Now, let's explore the ethereal domain of human emotions. In the mosaic of life, emotions are the hues that add depth and dimension. Embracing them is like letting the colors bleed onto the canvas. Acknowledging our feelings, even the painful ones, is the first step toward healing. It's like stitching up the frayed edges of a tapestry. By allowing ourselves to experience our emotions fully, we clear a path for the healing process to begin.

In the realm of resilience, self-care is the secret elixir. It's like a sanctuary we build within ourselves, a space where we tend to our physical, mental, and emotional needs. Engaging in regular exercise, embracing relaxation techniques like yoga and meditation, getting adequate sleep, and nourishing our bodies with a balanced diet—these actions collectively fortify our resilience.

And amidst life's whirlwind, we find meaning and purpose in the very fundamental elements that sustain us. Indeed, there will be times when life seems to shovel dirt on us, reminiscent of the classic tale of the Donkey Story. In this narrative, a donkey finds itself in a challenging situation when dirt is piled onto its back. Yet, instead of succumbing to the burden, the donkey shakes it off and takes a step up. With each new layer of dirt, the donkey continues to shake it off and step up until it rises above the pit it's trapped in. By engaging in activities that bring us joy, we rekindle the flame of purpose within. Helping others, pursuing hobbies, and savoring small victories remind us that life challenges are just chapters in a larger narrative.

But perhaps the greatest testament to resilience lies in staying motivated. In the face of adversity, perseverance becomes our compass, guiding us through the darkest nights. Resilience is like the hand that reaches out to pull us from the abyss. It's the unwavering determination to overcome challenges, no matter how daunting they may be. Taking small steps, celebrating even the tiniest victories, and nurturing an optimistic outlook are the tools that kindle the flame of motivation within us.

In this beautiful symphony of resilience, it is vital to keep in mind that there is no room for self-judgment. Similar to the growth of a bamboo plant, it takes time and dedication to establish strong roots before shooting up rapidly. Each individual has their own rhythm, gracefully facing challenges in their own unique way and patiently building a solid foundation. These efforts are vital to every success story, quietly working behind the scenes before visible growth and achievement. Ultimately, at the core of it all, we must have self-compassion and understand that it is perfectly okay to stumble as long as we continue to make progress.

V. Positive Thoughts Create Positive Outcomes

❖ Positive Thoughts and the Law of Attraction

Japanese Shinto Gobusho's[13] sage insight unveils the idea that beneath our individuality lies an ethereal unity, a universal essence. This essence is where the Law of Attraction finds its footing. It operates on the premise that

[13] "Shinto Gobusho" was a foundational book of Ise Shinto (also known as Watarai Shinto— a school of Shinto thought established by priests of the Grand Shrine of Ise in the medieval period) and a collective term for the following five-volume apologia.

while every person's journey is unique, fundamental laws exist that govern us all. These laws dictate that our experiences are intimately linked to the thoughts we nurture.

Furthermore, they underscore the idea that each of us is intrinsically tied to a wellspring of boundless energy— a constant flow of love and appreciation. This interconnectedness with the cosmic energy source presents us with a remarkable opportunity: the ability to shape our own destiny, manifest our desires, and bask in abundance. All of this becomes attainable when we focus on positivity and gratitude, opening the channels to tap into this cosmic energy and fostering a deeper connection with ourselves and the vast world around us.

❖ Authenticity as the Path to Fulfillment

The journey towards success is often navigated with the compass of authenticity. It is the guiding principle that reveals our unique purpose and sets the stage for a meaningful life. When we align ourselves with our genuine aspirations, the universe responds in kindness. It conspires to provide precisely what we seek when we need it most. This alignment propels us into higher states of consciousness and self-awareness, lifting us out of the stagnant routine of existence.

As we walk the path of authenticity, we find ourselves drawn closer to our life's true purpose. The result is a profound sense of happiness and a life teeming with meaning. Moreover, this journey into authenticity enhances our connections with others. Carl Rogers eloquently described how our most private and personal feelings often resonate deeply with others. By accepting the uniqueness of every individual, we find ourselves accepted in return for our own singular essence. This acceptance allows us to feel a sense of belonging, knowing that we fit in, no matter where we are. It also encourages us to celebrate our differences, knowing that our unique qualities and perspectives will be valued and embraced.

❖ Feelings as an Intuitive Guide

Sometimes, our journey is marked by an unmistakable sense of direction – an intuitive pull that guides us forward with unwavering certainty. Even great minds like Albert Einstein acknowledged the role of these emotional responses in their creative processes. They are the emotional precursors to rational understanding or gut feeling.

The Law of Attraction tells us that each individual possesses a personal wellspring of unique guidance in the form of feelings. These feelings act as a compass that guides us toward our deepest desires and aspirations. Although intuition seems vague, the famous psychiatrists Dr. Viktor Frankl of Vienna and Dr. Karl Menninger, when asked, "What is intuition?"? Their answer was simple and honest: "No one knows.

The psychiatrist Scott Peck pointed out in his book "The Road Less Travelled" that "The subconscious is always ahead of the conscious" to believe that your ideas are worthwhile. And have confidence in your God-given instincts. More often than not, they will be right.

❖ Manifestation and Meditation[14]

Every dream we conceive is born instantaneously in the boundless realm of energy. To bring these dreams into the tangible world, we must cultivate positive thoughts. Meditation emerges as a powerful tool in this endeavor, as it clears the mind, making it more receptive to the guidance of our inner feelings. Through meditation, we elevate our vibrational frequency, drawing our desires closer to us in our lives.

Meditation involves being present within, typically sitting still and focusing on your breath. However, your mind may wander, but gently bring it back. With practice, staying focused feels good, and distractions become less frequent, creating a sense of peace. It's similar to when cows are released from a barn after being confined for a while - initially, they run around, but eventually, they calm down and feel at peace.

❖ Interpretation of Preferences

During wakefulness, our subconscious mind often communicates with us in a subtle and benevolent manner, much like it does during sleep, albeit in a slightly different way. This communication takes the form of "idle thoughts"

---

[14] Meditation is a practice of mindfulness, and focusing the mind on a particular object, thought, or activity to train attention and awareness, and achieve a mentally clear, emotionally calm, and stable state. Meditation is practiced in numerous religious traditions. The earliest records of meditation (*dhyana*) are found in the Upanishads, and meditation plays a vital role in Hinduism, Jainism, and Buddhism. Since the 19th century, Asian meditative techniques have been adopted by other cultures, where they have also found applications in non-spiritual contexts, such as business and healthcare. Meditation may significantly reduce stress, anxiety, depression, and pain, and enhance peace, perception, self-concept, and well-being. Research is ongoing to understand better the effects of meditation on health (psychological, neurological, and cardiovascular) and other areas.

or even fragments of thought. Regrettably, much like how we often dismiss dreams, we tend to ignore and cast aside these idle thoughts, assuming they lack any meaningful significance.

Taking a deeper look at our preferences reveals the subtleties of our individuality. By examining the reasons behind our likes and dislikes, we uncover intricate details about ourselves as unique beings. These preferences are not mere whims; they are the echoes of our soul's song, resonating with the core of our individuality.

VI. What Goes Around Comes Around

The age-old saying, "What goes around comes around," encapsulates the ethos of a universal truth—Karma. This mysterious principle teaches us that the consequences of our actions are not fleeting; they are destined to return to us in due course. It serves as a poignant reminder of the uncanny interconnectedness of our choices and their enduring effects on our lives.

❖ The Law of Attraction and Accountability

At the heart of the concept of "what goes around comes around" lies the Law of Attraction, which posits that our thoughts and deeds are inextricably linked to our experiences. Throughout our lives, the decisions we make have profound implications for our future. Hence, it becomes our solemn duty to exercise prudence and contemplate the long-term repercussions of our choices. Every action we take and every decision we make has its consequences, which we must be willing to embrace and take responsibility for.

❖ The Boomerang Effect of Actions

Much like the trajectory of a boomerang, our actions are bound to return to us. In essence, we must be cautious and deliberate in our actions, ensuring that they radiate positivity and goodwill. The wisdom echoed by *Roy T Bennett* serves as a guiding light in this regard: "*Treat everyone with politeness and kindness, not because they are nice, but because you are.*" By cultivating a spirit of kindness, mindfulness, and respect for others, we contribute to a virtuous cycle of positive actions that ultimately shape our destiny.

❖ Karma: The Cosmic Balance and Mysteries

Delving deeper into the realms of Karma, we encounter an enigmatic cosmic principle—the law of cause and effect. This principle, often distilled into the adage "as you sow, so shall you reap," underscores the incomprehensible interplay between our actions and their consequences. It classifies Karma into four categories: good, bad, individual, and collective, with each action yielding its respective fruits.

Yet, when life takes unexpected and bewildering turns, we are left grappling for answers. Three plausible explanations arise— divine cruelty, random chaos, or the notion that we might have unknowingly contributed to our suffering. The third option, hinted at by the Bhagavad Gita, invites us to shoulder responsibility for our actions, acknowledging their ripple effect across lifetimes.

Karma, however, is not a swift reckoning; it operates on its own cosmic timetable. It manifests when the universe deems it fit, sometimes even accumulating multiple reactions—positive or negative—before delivering its judgment. This process is akin to a credit card bill that accumulates over time, becoming payable at a later date.

- **Breaking the Cycle of Karma through Conscious Action**

The question often arises: "Why should we be held accountable for actions from past lives that we cannot recall?" This query not only underscores the inherent complexity of Karma but also the importance of mindfulness in our present actions. As the Bhagavad Gita and Hinduism emphasize, by cultivating awareness in our current actions and gradually dissipating the karmic reactions we've amassed, we can pave the way for a prosperous future, both materially and spiritually.

However, Karma should never be misconstrued as an excuse for indifference to the suffering of others. Compassion and empathy should always take precedence. The cycle of action and reaction can be broken through Bhakti Yoga, which incorporates mantra meditation, conscious eating, and devotional service. It offers a path to transcend the material world, alleviate karmic burdens, and attain spiritual consciousness.

VII. You Fail, Only If You Quit

Success often waits in the shadows to reveal itself at the right moment. It's a truth that we might not fully understand success until we fail. In the pursuit of our goals and aspirations, we often encounter a multifaceted process, one in which success is knitted with the threads of failure. It's a paradoxical truth that success is not merely the absence of failure but a culmination of tenacity, perseverance, and resilience. In this journey, the adage

"You fail only if you quit" takes center stage, serving as a beacon of wisdom.

❖ The Triumph of Tenacity

Success, in its truest form, is born from the willingness to venture, to try, and sometimes, to fail. Failure, far from being a roadblock, is a stepping stone on the path to success. Think of a pole vaulter as an example. Their path to success is anything but easy. It's not about winning as soon as they jump over the bar; rather, the true nature of success shows itself when they fall short of the greatest challenge. In a strange way, loss is the first step to success. It's through these failures that we glean invaluable lessons and emerge as individuals who are not only stronger but also wiser. Being focused on the game you're in, rather than dwelling on the past or worrying about the future, is essential for success. The great news is that you can transform your failures into investments. It's true! Have you experienced setbacks? Many people would like to know why. Capitalize on their curiosity! Consider becoming a consultant!

❖ Unveiling the Essence of Effort

In our pursuit of success, it's easy to focus solely on the end result, attributing triumph to the 1% that represents achievement while inadvertently neglecting the 99% that constitutes effort. Yet, it is essential to recognize that without the entirety of this endeavor, we cannot truly appreciate the value of that final 1%. Every ounce of effort, even if it doesn't yield the desired outcome, is an integral and valuable part of success. "Success is 99% failure."!

These experiences, often seen as setbacks, are, in fact, the crucibles in which we forge our work ethic and determination. They impart invaluable lessons, becoming the bedrock upon which we build our future endeavors. Successful individuals and businesses understand the art of capitalizing on these experiences, mining the 1% from the 99% and transforming it into their unique advantage.

❖ The Journey to the Summit

Success, akin to ascending a formidable mountain, is a journey of a thousand steps. There are moments when progress seems imperceptible and when it feels like we are merely treading water. Sustaining your commitment to the journey also hinges on how you approach goal setting. Consistency and persistence in the goals you select are vital, but it's equally important to detach your happiness from the ultimate outcome you seek. If you tie your happiness solely to achieving a specific goal, you risk fixating on the future rather than finding inspiration in the present. Instead, aim to build momentum by initially setting achievable goals and gradually increasing the level of effort as you make progress. One step at a time, no matter how small or seemingly insignificant, will help you stay focused and motivated on your path to personal success.

In the words of motivational speaker Therone Shellman, "*It's not so important what you accomplish, but what's more important is how far you've come to accomplish what you have.*" The end result does not solely define success; it is equally a reflection of the unwavering determination and hard work invested along the way.

❖ Celebrating Every Step

Every stride toward our goals, no matter how modest it may appear, is a cause for celebration. These small victories, when acknowledged and cherished, can trigger a domino effect[15], propelling us toward more extensive and more significant achievements. Progress, regardless of its scale, is still progress, and each step forward carries its unique merit. The quest for success isn't only about reaching big goals, but it's also about getting to know yourself and growing as a person. It's about knowing what you're good at and having the guts to go after it.

VIII. Judgements are a Confession of Character

Our judgments of others serve as revealing portraits of our inner selves. Like mirrors reflecting our thoughts and emotions, they lay bare the intricacies of our biases, the contours of our beliefs, and the colors of our values. In each judgment, we unveil a piece of our identity, exposing how we perceive the world and the values that guide us.

It's paramount to recognize that our judgments are not impartial assessments but rather the product of our unique life experiences, cultural influences, and personal perspectives. They carry the weight of our beliefs and biases, often hidden beneath the surface of seemingly objective opinions.

To cultivate fairness and wisdom in our judgments, we must embark on a journey of self-awareness. We must acknowledge our inherent biases and be vigilant against letting them cloud our judgment. By actively seeking diverse perspectives and taking the time to consider alternative viewpoints, we can rise above the limitations of

[15] A ***domino effect*** or chain reaction is the cumulative effect produced when one event sets off a chain of similar events. This term is best known as a mechanical effect and is used as an analogy to a falling row of dominoes. It typically refers to a linked sequence of events where the time between successive events is relatively small.

our own subjectivity. Wisdom often remains obscured by a veil of ignorance, and the true expression of wisdom occurs when this veil is lifted. It's akin to a dusty mirror concealed under layers of grime. Only when the dust is cleared away can the mirror reflect the entirety of the universe.

Moreover, we must be acutely aware of the impact our judgments can have on others. Each judgment carries the potential to shape the way others perceive themselves and their place in the world. This realization obliges us to approach judgment with respect and empathy, mindful of the emotions and dignity of those we evaluate.

The eyes are for navigation, like the headlights of a car, to show you the way. Not to judge what you see, so True character is revealed not in the act of judgment itself but in our willingness to learn and grow. To foster personal growth, we must remain open to changing our opinions when presented with new evidence or fresh perspectives. We should embrace humility and place ourselves in the shoes of those we assess, striving to understand their experiences and motivations.

The wisdom encapsulated in the adage "*judge not, lest you be judged.*" To be compassionate judges of character, we should aspire to positively influence the world around us, seeking to uplift others rather than condemn them. And amidst the seriousness of life, we mustn't forget to laugh at ourselves, for it is laughter that reminds us of our shared humanity and the imperfections that make us beautifully human.

IX. Overthinking Causes Sadness

When we overthink, we ruminate on negative thoughts, which can lead to feelings of hopelessness and despair. This can eventually spiral into a cycle of negative thinking and depression. It is important to recognize when we are overthinking and take steps to stop it before it leads to sadness. We can practice mindfulness and focus on the present moment. We can also talk to a friend or do an activity to help distract us from overthinking. Ultimately, we can cultivate self-compassion and be kind to ourselves when we find ourselves caught in a cycle of negative thinking.

Negative thought cycles are like quicksand. The more you try to struggle against it, the deeper it sucks you in. Taking control of your thoughts is like using a rope to pull yourself out of quicksand – it requires conscious effort and patience, but it can be done. AS *Roy T Bennett once said*: *"Do not let your negative thoughts have power over you because those thoughts will end up controlling your life. No one can live a positive life with a negative mind."* The key to taking control of our thoughts is to become aware of them and recognize when our mind is jumping to conclusions or dwelling on something negative. We can then consciously choose to challenge those thoughts and reframe them in a positive light. This will help us break free from our negative thought patterns and become more aware of our thinking.

Everybody gets too deep in their heads about things, and we've all been caught up in the never-ending cycle of the "what ifs?"

What if I can't afford it? What if they aren't fond of me? What if this change worsens things?

There's a difference between thinking the right amount and overthinking. Our brains are amazing processors, and we make conscious and subconscious decisions 40,000 times per day. Careful analysis and scrutiny can lead to confident choices, but excessive worrying and analysis can have the opposite effect.

The question is, when is an inquisitive nature helpful, and when does overthinking become an issue? Do you really have any control over this?

❖ **How do you know if you're overthinking?**

One thing to realize about overthinking is how much it resembles the problem-solving process. But the two are definitely distinct.

"Problem-solving is when you ask questions with the intent of finding an answer or enacting a solution." "Overthinking, on the other hand, is when you dwell on possibilities and pitfalls without any real intent of solving a problem. In fact, a problem or potential problem may not be present at all."

❖ **Overthinking can also feel like self-reflection, but both are distinct**

"Self-reflection is an internally inquisitive process rooted in a higher purpose—whether that's to grow as a person or gain a new perspective. If you're obsessing over something you don't like about yourself that you either can't change or have no intention of improving, it's not self-reflection—it's overthinking."

Still, overthinking can be tricky to spot. Signs of overthinking include:

- Reminiscing about the past
- Doubting your decisions
- Mentally replaying your mistakes

- Rehashing difficult or uncomfortable conversations
- Being fixated on things you can't control, improve, or change
- Creating a worst-case scenario
- You focus on your fears in the unalterable past or unforeseeable future rather than in the present moment
- While trying to fall asleep, you are "running your list."
- Questioning but never deciding or acting

❖ **How does overthinking affect you?**

While it may feel like overthinking is just something that happens in your head, it's more than that.

Overthinking disrupts the way you engage with the world around you, prevents you from making the appropriate choices, and drains your energy. When you dwell on the past or catastrophize about the future, your mental and physical health can be compromised.

Studies have shown that ruminating on stressful events can lead to anxiety and depression over time."

"Anxiety affects your ability to cope with everyday stressors, while depression causes sadness, loneliness, and emptiness."

❖ **What to do when overthinking hits**

When you catch yourself second-guessing your decision or imagining the worst-case scenario, try these tips to prevent overthinking:

- **Don't sweat the small stuff**

You already know this, but it needs to be said: Of the thousands of decisions you make every day, the majority are simply not worth draining your brain power over.

Consider your priorities and what is meaningful to you when identifying the decisions that are worth careful consideration. By doing so, you can determine when to embrace your inquisitive, perfectionist nature and when to refrain from critical thinking, scrutiny, and skepticism.

- **Think critically and act instinctively**

When making a significant decision, it's easy to become consumed by obsessing over the possibilities and potential pitfalls. Do your research, ask questions, and collect facts, but don't be afraid to trust your gut.

And remember that logical problem-solving is not always a cure-all.

It can sometimes be more accurate to sign in with your intuition or gut than to be slow and deliberate." "While neither approach is foolproof, snap decisions open up the implicit processing capacity of your mind and help disrupt your ruminations."

- **Take a break or set a deadline**

If you give yourself too much time to think about a decision, you're more likely to overanalyze it.

When solving a problem, set a deadline for making your final decision. If the decision-making process becomes overwhelming, consider taking breaks to distract yourself.

❖ **Let go of what you can't control and act on what you can**

In the event that you become lost in your own thoughts about something, ask yourself if you can transform them into something more constructive, such as deciding or finding a solution.

If your thought pattern isn't constructive, you're likely dwelling on something out of your control, whether it has already happened, may never happen, or can't be changed. Consider letting go of these negative thoughts.

We can't control or change all aspects of life, just as gravity cannot be undone. Focusing instead on the aspects we can change can help us let go of the unsolvable."

Beyond your general temperament, which we know is genetically determined, if you are naturally high-strung and easily perturbed, consider trying yoga and meditation to help mitigate your reactivity.

X. Kindness is Free

Kindness, often defined as the quality of being friendly, generous, and considerate, holds a far deeper meaning than mere dictionary entries suggest. It's an abstract yet profound concept that transcends words, encompassing a vast spectrum of human emotions, actions, and intentions.

The beauty of kindness lies in its versatility. Each individual can uniquely express it through empathy, acceptance, thoughtful gestures, or selfless acts. It's not a one-size-fits-all virtue but a flexible canvas upon which we paint our intentions. Expectations of reciprocity don't bind kindness; it flows freely from the heart, expecting nothing in return.

It's essential to distinguish between being merely "nice" and embodying true kindness. Niceness can sometimes lack depth, with its actions appearing superficial and obligatory. Kindness, on the other hand, involves deliberate, voluntary acts driven by empathy, compassion, and an unwavering commitment to making a positive impact, even in the face of challenges.

One of the most remarkable aspects of kindness is its ripple effect. Have you ever experienced a simple act of kindness that inspired you to pay it forward? This is the magic of kindness—a single act can set in motion a chain reaction, fostering positivity and compassion in our communities. As Mahatma Gandhi wisely proclaimed, "*Be the change you wish to see in the world.*" It's a testament to the transformative power of individual kindness that can extend far beyond the initial act.

At its core, kindness is closely tied to love. The profound essence of love—selflessness, care, compassion—is reflected in every act of kindness we bestow upon others. When we offer a smile, lend an encouraging word, perform an unexpected deed, or plan a surprise for someone, we share love in its purest form. Kindness becomes the vessel through which love flows, radiating positivity, inspiring hope, and promoting peace.

Moreover, kindness extends to ourselves. As humans, we are bound to make mistakes; in these moments, kindness can act as our guiding light. It means pausing to reflect before reacting, choosing forgiveness over revenge, and prioritizing long-term relationships over fleeting pride. Embracing our imperfections and offering ourselves the grace to grow and learn is an act of self-kindness that nourishes the soul.

One remarkable aspect of kindness is that it is entirely free of charge. Unlike many endeavors that require time or financial resources, kindness is a universally accessible currency of compassion. Small, simple gestures can yield significant impacts, and the wellspring of kindness resides within us, waiting to be shared with the world.

The benefits of kindness aren't one-sided. Research suggests that individuals who engage in spontaneous acts of kindness often experience enhanced happiness, which is often rooted in a sense of autonomy and deeper interpersonal connections. Kindness contributes to a sense of meaning and purpose in life, transcending the fleeting pleasures of hedonistic happiness. It involves effort and sacrifice, which, in turn, can boost self-esteem, self-efficacy, and overall well-being.

Imagine a world where every individual practices one act of kindness daily, creating a tapestry of compassion that counterbalances the negativity we encounter. The beauty of kindness is that it's a gift that keeps on giving—both the giver and receiver benefit, and the entire world becomes a better place. The Dalai Lama encapsulated this truth when he said, "*If you want others to be happy, practice compassion. If you want to be happy, practice compassion.*" In this simple yet profound notion, we find the universal virtue of helping others an economical way to enhance both the well-being of others and our own. Kindness, a timeless and boundless virtue, has the power to shape a world where compassion reigns supreme.

(Numerous outstanding leaders possess the qualities of selfless kindness and compassion in their leadership approach.)[16]

XI. Smile is Contagious

A smile, often underestimated in its simplicity, possesses an incredible power to illuminate the world around us. It can transform the atmosphere in a room, elevate the spirits of those nearby, and even radiate joy to those miles away. This seemingly small gesture costs us nothing and holds immeasurable value for both the giver and the receiver.

A smile possesses the enchanting ability to brighten someone's day, transcending even the darkest moments. It serves as a universal symbol of warmth, an unspoken language of kindness that transcends boundaries and circumstances. It's a gesture that knows no bounds, a connection established in an instant, and is the shortest distance between people. It acts as a bridge that brings people closer, breaking down barriers that might otherwise impede human interaction. A smile has the amazing ability not only to facilitate social connections but also to create a sense of ease, comfort, and trust in others.

Beyond its immediate effects, scientific studies have unveiled the intangible impact of smiling on our well-being. A simple smile triggers the release of endorphins, those delightful little chemicals that enhance our mood and

[16] For example, Mother Teresa chose to leave her home country and devote herself to serving the impoverished and needy people of India. Albert Schweitzer also sacrificed a comfortable life in France to assist the less fortunate in Africa. Similarly, Henry Dunant relinquished his prosperous business to aid those affected by the war and establish the International Committee of the Red Cross, now known as the Red Cross movement. Nelson Mandela endured twenty-seven years of imprisonment in his fight against South African apartheid. The 14th Dalai Lama, despite being in exile from his homeland, Tibet, has become a symbol of global peace and harmony. These are just a few examples, among many others.

alleviate stress. It's a natural mood booster that benefits the person smiling and spreads positivity to those around them. It fortifies our physical health by boosting the immune system, contributing to a more resilient body. Simultaneously, it bolsters self-confidence, making us feel better about ourselves and our interactions with others. It even enhances our appeal, making us more attractive to those around us.

During my time in Mumbai, I made it a habit to count how many people were smiling during my morning commute on the local. The thought of what I was doing always made me smile. Then, I would look around the cart again and count all the people I infected with my smile. I tried my very best to make it a cheerful smile. Not the creepy kind. I loved the idea. After a year of consistently doing this, I genuinely believe I made all these mornings a little brighter and all these strangers a little happier. I could establish the correlation between my smile, the weather, weekdays, train delays, and the smiles of others.

"When traveling, one realizes one thing quite quickly: a smile can change everything. It can open doors and the hearts of other people whose culture you do not even know. A smile is the global language that everyone knows." Smile from the inside. It will leave you with an overall positive feeling and help you smile more often. Then, others will smile back at you. I love how contagious smiles are. I make a concerted effort to smile at others.

The enchantment of a smile does not only come from its immediate impact but also from the long-lasting benefits it brings to one's psychological well-being. As a motivational speaker, Gillian Duce beautifully articulated, "*A smile is a light within you being turned on; it can illuminate the path for you and others.*"

In our fast-paced lives, we often underestimate the simplicity of a smile and its potential to brighten our world. Children, on average, smile about 400 times a day, while adults, on average, smile only 40 to 50 times daily when they are happy. It's a reminder that the universal language of kindness is always at our disposal, ready to transcend barriers and spread warmth and light to the world.

XII. Happiness Begins Within

Happiness isn't something we find outside of ourselves; it's a choice we make from deep within. To truly embrace happiness, we must begin by looking within ourselves, recognizing our core values, and paying attention to our inner thoughts and feelings. This inner journey forms the basis for creating a life that genuinely reflects who we are.

In our pursuit of happiness, we often overlook our simple yet precious moments. These moments hold the key to our contentment. By learning to appreciate these simple pleasures, we can uncover the happiness that already surrounds us. It's in the laughter of a loved one, the beauty of a sunrise, or the peace of a quiet moment that we catch glimpses of happiness. So, don't sacrifice "today" for an imaginary tomorrow.

Gratitude also plays a vital role in nurturing our inner happiness. Instead of focusing on what we lack, we should concentrate on what we have. Cultivating a mindset of gratitude enables us to appreciate the present and acknowledge the abundance already present in our lives.

The COVID-19 pandemic probably helped us realize that even to keep breathing is a miracle. So, waking up alive the next day is happiness because the moment we are born, we are really beginning to die, and the decay of our bodies could be a cause of our misery.

I challenge any of you to describe to me happiness, for instance. You can only say, "I am Happy. And if I ask why? The answer could be the temporal level, which refers to any favorable condition related to the job, relationships, or any other specific achievement at that point in time that might change sooner or later. Conditioned happiness is no happiness! If you are conditioned in your happiness, you might feel miserable again after the condition is removed.

Life's existence often presents itself as a formidable test, characterized by arduous trials, disheartening disappointments, and seemingly insurmountable barriers. Tragically, no effortless panacea exists to alleviate our burdens or dismantle the intricate framework that sustains our being. Nevertheless, it is imperative that we adopt a consistent methodology to alleviate our sorrows. Through indulging in captivating diversions, redirecting our attention, and discovering alternative avenues for satisfaction or respite, we can find solace amidst the tumultuous journey of life.

So, embracing happiness as a habit means moving away from the misconception that it's tied to success, material possessions, or the unbridled gratification of desires. It's more of a practice - a conscious decision to focus on life's positive aspects. It involves actively seeking joy, celebrating even small victories, and learning from our failures.

Taking risks, although intimidating at times, can be a catalyst for personal growth and fulfillment. Stepping out of our comfort zones and embracing change can open doors to new opportunities and fresh perspectives. It's often in the face of uncertainty that we discover our hidden strengths and capabilities. But at times, we set our course, and a wind blows us off course!

We all know about Chernobyl, which is considered safe and beneficial for the Russians. A minor disaster occurred. God's grace saved us from a major catastrophe. The reason I give this example is that even the most experienced driver in the best car on the smoothest roads can have what we call an "accident." By definition, no accident is intentional, no accident is desired, and no accident ever has desirable results. It makes sense to have a controlled, regulated, and willed existence. Furthermore, a life filled with happiness doesn't demand perfection but rather the acceptance of our imperfections. Each of us is on a unique journey, akin to a roller coaster ride, with both highs and lows contributing to our growth and self-discovery. Just as the anticipation and thrill of the climb make a roller coaster ride enjoyable, it's the entire journey that enriches our lives. The journey, with its twists and turns, ups and downs, is where we accumulate wisdom, broaden our horizons, and create lasting memories. It's through this journey that we evolve, gain insight, and build resilience.

In our pursuit of happiness, let's remember that it's not a distant destination to reach but a habit to nurture. By focusing on our inner values, cherishing life's simplicity, practicing gratitude, embracing change, and celebrating the entire journey, we can cultivate a life where happiness flourishes from within. A flight is Successful not when it takes off but only when it lands safely on the other side. So, probably, it is at the end of life that we must judge how we have lived. So, having a long-term perspective is a deeply insightful viewpoint, acknowledging that making a lasting difference often spans a lifetime. As we navigate life's unpredictable terrain, it's vital to remember that the challenges we encounter today are just chapters in a much larger and more intricate story.

Our struggles don't define us; they refine us! Much like carboniferous forests under enormous pressure, they have the potential to transform us. Just as trees, under pressure, become coal, and under heat and pressure, they become diamonds, we too evolve through the crucible of adversity. This transformation doesn't come without heat and pressure. Still, through acceptance, self-care, purpose, and unwavering determination, we rise from the ashes of adversity, emerging as more robust, wiser, and more resilient individuals, much like the diamonds that emerge from the depths of the Earth's pressure.

Each day, our lives are brimming with opportunities that often disguise themselves within ordinary or routine situations. While these opportunities may seem unremarkable, they have the potential to inch us closer to our goals. They might manifest as challenges, delays, or even encounters with unexpected individuals. The crucial skill lies in recognizing and seizing these opportunities, thereby transforming the ordinary into the extraordinary. By remaining attuned to the daily opportunities that surround us and by leveraging failures as stepping stones, we can unlock our genuine potential and draw ourselves nearer to the success that has always been within our grasp.

Each of these **"Twelve hypotheses"** serves as a teacher, a molder, and a stepping stone, propelling us toward a brighter tomorrow. This journey unfolds gradually, inviting us not only to embrace its lessons and celebrate its victories but also to become the architects of our own resilience. By understanding the enduring nature of our life's narrative, we gain the wisdom to persist, adapt, and make a meaningful impact over the course of our journey.

***

CHAPTER-2

The Paragons of Leadership

—UNCONVENTIONAL LEADERS

- **New Leadership Equation**

It is essential to acquire a refined leadership perspective in light of our ever-changing environment. This strategy must effectively guide us through uncertain times, interconnected global networks, decentralized frameworks, and rising demands from employees and customers for moral principles and meaningful goals. To meet these requirements, innovative concepts, a reevaluation of fundamental convictions, and the incorporation of progressive values are necessary.

Consider leadership to be a new equation. It's similar to taking an alternative route to address an issue. We must think creatively as if tackling a puzzle from a different angle. Because the world has changed, we must be prepared to adjust our course in response to the unmet needs of human beings. We must reconsider leadership and explore how it relates to the changing reality.

This new leadership paradigm should emphasize today's values, including honesty, justice, and a sense of purpose. It's not only about being the boss; it's about leading a team through today's obstacles. So, let us not get caught up in the

Past. Let us rethink leadership in light of our changing world.

- **Role Model?**
  When IQ and EQ are Embedded with SQ

Leadership Quotient (LQ) is a unique trait possessed by exceptional leaders, which is a mix of several vital components: Intelligence (IQ), Emotional Intelligence (EQ), Physical Health (PQ), and Spiritual Insight (SQ). When we combine, we get what we call a "role model." Robert K. Merton[17] invented this phrase to describe someone who acts as a model for others by exhibiting different ideals and actions that encourage emulation. It is essential to recognize that a role model is not a perfect replica, but rather symbolizes a partial identification with key responsibilities and attributes.

[17] **Robert King Merton** (July 1910-February 2003) was an American sociologist who is credited with founding modern sociology and making significant contributions to criminology. He served as the 47th president of the American Sociological Association. He spent most of his career teaching at Columbia University and attained the rank of university professor. In 1994, he was awarded the National Medal of Science for his contributions to the field and for having founded the sociology of science. Merton's contributions to sociology fall into three areas: the sociology of science, the sociology of crime and deviance, and sociological theory. He developed notable concepts such as "unintended consequences," the "reference group," and "role strain," but is perhaps best known for the terms **"role model"** and "self-fulfilling prophecy." The concept of self-fulfilling prophecy, a central element in modern sociological, political, and economic theory, is one type of process through which a belief or expectation affects the outcome of a situation or the way a person or group behaves. More specifically, as Merton defined, "the self-fulfilling prophecy is, in the beginning, a false definition of the situation evoking a new behaviour, which makes the originally false conception come true." The term originated from his theory of the reference group, which is the group to which individuals compare themselves, but to which they do not necessarily belong. Merton emphasized that, rather than a person assuming just one role and one status, they have a status set in the social structure that has attached to it a whole set of expected behaviors.

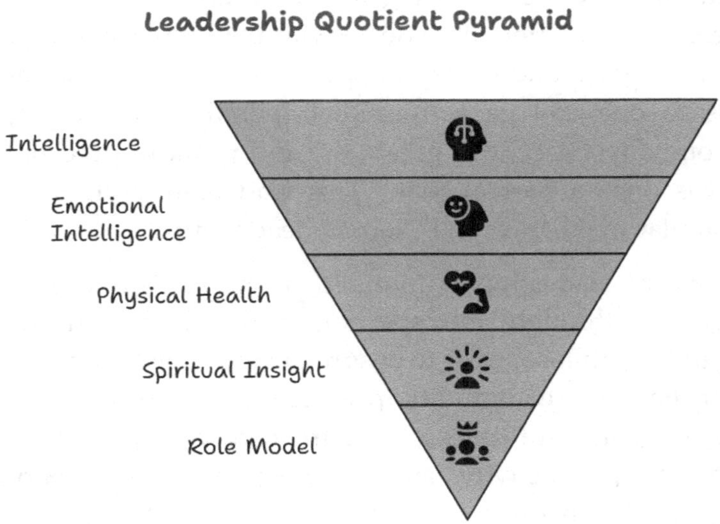

Our parents are frequently our first role models during our early years. They form many of our beliefs and actions, laying the groundwork for us to comprehend the world. The amazing thing about our brains, though, is their plasticity. Our brain's neuronal circuitry may be molded and rewired thanks to a phenomenon known as neuroplasticity. This means that, even if we inherit many of our parents' values and behavior patterns, we have the ability to accept new role models and change the trajectory of our lives.

Throughout history, exceptional leaders with distinctive habits and ideals have forged a tradition of leaving an indelible mark on society, providing inspiration for generations to come. These visionary leaders are not motivated by personal gain but rather by the enduring prosperity of their organizations. They consistently identify and nurture exceptional successors, with the ultimate goal of ensuring the continued success of their companies. Often, they do so with the understanding that their contributions may go uncelebrated. Their aspiration is to one day gaze from their porch, witnessing their company's ascent to greatness, and proudly proclaim, "I was once a part of that." This leadership style is quite similar to what we call "Servant leadership."

Servant leadership is founded on humanistic principles gained through introspection and self-awareness. Its guiding philosophy is to ensure the well-being and success of the entire community, prioritizing people over profits. This approach fosters greater trust, enhances morale, and boosts productivity among those being led. Servant leadership is distinguished by its persistent emphasis on the common good, making it a highly effective and influential approach to managing and inspiring others.

Ultimately, outstanding leaders possess a high Leadership Quotient (LQ) that encompasses several key characteristics. Robert K. Merton's concept of role models emphasizes the relevance of emulation and the plasticity of the brain's neural architecture. Throughout history, unconventional leaders have encouraged us to prioritize the greater good —a mindset that aligns with current servant leadership, characterized by its dedication to human welfare and community success.

In today's society, one could possibly describe role models as being somewhat unconventional. "Leaders!! The most powerfully transformative executives possess a paradoxical mixture of personal humility and professional will.

They are Timid and Ferocious. Shy and Fearless. They are Rare— and Unstoppable."

- **Unconventional Leaders— The "Eleven Traits"**

In today's environment, role models are frequently Unconventional Leaders. These leaders break the mold and redefine success, changing the paradigm of leadership in modern culture.

In the traditional world, leadership success is typically measured by the magnitude of visible achievements – revenues generated, and power accumulated. The prevailing belief is that the most effective leader is the one who can deliver the most tangible results, regardless of the techniques employed. Henry Ford, Steve Jobs, and Jack Welch are just a few examples. What binds these legendary leaders together? It's their extraordinary triumph, the type that reverberates across history. They were recognized for their capacity to produce results and achieve greatness through unique and creative techniques. Their ability to think outside the box and create game-changing ideas transformed their respective industries. Their unwavering pursuit of greatness catapulted them to victory.

Other names, maybe less well-known, are Colman M. Mockler, Darwin E. Smith, and George Cain. While these names may not immediately spring to mind, they, too, achieved extraordinary success, albeit in different ways. What distinguishes them is their unconventional approach to leadership and their unique techniques for achieving their objectives.

Jim Collins[18] **A** renowned leadership specialist offers the concept of "Level-5" leadership, which only a few people possess. Being a "Level-5" leader entails more than eccentricity or foresight. It is a significant divergence from the traditional leadership approach. These leaders have a unique combination of humility and tenacity. Rather than seeking personal recognition or financial gain, they direct their energy toward the success of their organizations. Their dedication to a higher purpose extends beyond money and power.

Colman M. Mockler, for example, guided **Gillette**[19] through a challenging phase by prioritizing the company's long-term interests ahead of short-term earnings. By concentrating on the company's fundamental ideals and principles, Darwin E. Smith built **Kimberly-Clark**[20], a stodgy old paper company, into a powerhouse, outperforming venerable companies such as Hewlett-

[18] **James C. "Jim" Collins** (born 1958) is an American researcher, author, speaker, and consultant focused on the subject of business management and company sustainability and growth.

[19] **Gillette,** founded by King C. Gillette in 1901, is an American brand of safety razors and other personal care products, including shaving supplies, owned by the multi-national corporation Procter & Gamble (P&G). Under the leadership of **Colman M. Mockler** Jr. as CEO from 1975 to 1991, the company was the target of multiple takeover attempts from Ronald Perelman and Coniston Partners. In January 2005, Procter & Gamble announced plans to merge with the Gillette Company.

[20] **Kimberly-Clark** is an American multinational corporation specializing in paper-based consumer products, including sanitary paper products and medical instruments. Notable brands include Kleenex, Kotex, Cottonelle, Scott, and Huggies. Founded in 1872 in Neenah, Wisconsin, and based in Irving, Texas since 1985, the company closed its last paper mills in 2012. With annual revenues exceeding $18 billion, it ranks among the Fortune 500 and employs around 40,000 people as of March 2020. Darwin Smith served as CEO from 1971 to 1991 and held degrees from Indiana University and Harvard Law School.

Packard, 3M, Coca-Cola, and General Electric. George Cain's unorthodox leadership at **Abbott Laboratories**[21] centred on cultivating a collaborative and innovative culture. These Unconventional Leaders exemplify a change in leadership ideals. They inspire others through their steadfast loyalty to their organizations and unshakable commitment to a higher purpose. Their legacy is characterized not just by financial metrics but also by their ability to foster cultures of innovation, integrity, and long-term success. They serve as role models in the modern world, demonstrating that leadership can extend beyond the pursuit of power and wealth, instead emphasizing the creation of lasting, positive societal benefits. Looking ahead, these Unconventional Leaders provide a roadmap for rethinking leadership success in a fast-changing world.

Let's explore the remarkable characteristics that define unconventional leaders.

---

[21] **Abbott Laboratories,** founded by Chicago physician Wallace Calvin Abbott in 1888, is an American multinational medical device and healthcare company with headquarters in Abbott Park, Illinois, United States. It split off its research-based pharmaceutical business into AbbVie in 2013. **Cain** joined Abbott, a pharmaceutical manufacturer with headquarters in North Chicago, in 1940. His first post was assistant sales manager of the hospital division. He became a director in 1947 and executive vice president in 1950. In 1965, as chairman of the Pharmaceutical Manufacturers Association at a time when prescription drug makers were undergoing public criticism, he acknowledged the problems of developing, evaluating, and introducing new drugs. He warned, nevertheless, that "delay and undue caution in administering drug regulations can kill and cripple people just as surely as haste and carelessness."

I. Prioritizes Others Over Self

Unconventional leaders possess distinctive qualities that distinguish them in the realm of leadership. They channel their ambition towards the success of the organization rather than self-aggrandizement, thus laying a solid foundation for the success of future generations. A notable trait of these leaders is their consistent prioritization of the needs and desires of others over their own, setting them apart. They operate quietly, employing subtle means to motivate and inspire their team members, in stark contrast to conventional leaders who seek the spotlight and personal accolades. Their unwavering commitment to the well-being and progress of their team underscores their genuine leadership qualities.

This kind of selfless leadership inspires leaders who don't follow the rules to take calculated risks and challenge established norms and habits. They are brave enough to accept new ideas and changes, and they want to bring growth and positive changes to their teams and organizations. This unique style of leadership has a profound and far-reaching impact, inspiring people to step out of their comfort zones and strive for greatness. A famous Nigerian motivational speaker, Fela Durotoye, said, "*Leadership is a serving relationship with others that inspires their growth and makes the world a better place.*" This is what unusual leadership is all about: setting a good example, encouraging growth, and making the world a better place.

However, in contrast, typical leaders tend to adhere to established rules and norms while also providing support to their teams. They encourage their team members to excel, but they may not always prioritize their well-being and contentment. On the contrary, leaders who deviate from the norm display a greater level of commitment towards their teams. They are willing to sacrifice their personal values, even if it means challenging conventional leadership standards.

Picture an unusual leader as a caring guardian figure for the team, much like a parent who prioritizes their children's needs. They are ready to take calculated risks and dedicate their time, effort, and resources to ensure that everyone on the team succeeds and thrives. This level of commitment can manifest in various ways, such as consistently being emotionally supportive of their team during challenging times or taking on additional tasks to make things easier for them. This kind of steadfast support from leaders who aren't typical is really priceless.

It's kind of like having a steady base in the middle of a storm; it keeps you safe and stable even when everything else is going wild. When things go wrong, knowing that someone is on your side and ready to help, and do whatever it takes to ensure your health and productivity, can make the difference between just living and thriving. This deep care for others is what makes unusual leaders stand out and helps their teams and organizations make progress and change for the better. Between 1975 and 1991, Gillette CEO Colman M. Mockler developed as a sturdy character, standing firm in the face of three hostile takeover bids. He possessed elegance and a distinctly aristocratic air, despite his guarded demeanor. When the storms of crisis raged around him, Mockler maintained the outward impression of business as usual, indicating a dedication to first ensuring regular corporate operations before dealing with the imminent danger of takeover.

Mockler and his other top executives embarked on a massive campaign to individually contact thousands of investors one by one in order to earn their votes in a high-stakes proxy contest. Rather than a hasty stock flip to earn personal money, he opted to fight tirelessly for Gillette's future glory. Mockler's decision has far-reaching consequences. The repercussions of his surrender would have been disastrous. Over the course of a decade, a shareholder who opted to stick with Mockler and Gillette would have come out 64% ahead of a share flipper who took Ronald Perelman's enticing 44% premium offer.

But Mockler's drive extended beyond monetary gain. His persistent determination ensured that innovations such as the Sensor, Lady Sensor, and Mach III razors came to fruition, improving the shaving experience for many people. Mockler's commitment saved hundreds of millions of people from having to deal with obstinate stubble on a regular basis. Regrettably, Colman M. Mockler could never fully enjoy the rewards of his tireless work. Fate took a tragic turn in January 1991. An early issue of Forbes arrived at Gillette, featuring a cover depicting an artist's portrayal of the publicity-shy Mockler proudly holding a giant razor aloft. Mockler, unfortunately, died of a severe heart attack minutes after getting this rare and public acknowledgment of his 16-year fight, leaving a legacy of leadership and commitment that would be remembered for decades to come.

II. Acknowledges Others and Absorbs Blame

Unconventional leaders have a distinct approach to managing praise and criticism, which sets them apart from the crowd. When confronted with unsatisfactory outcomes, they look in the mirror and gladly accept responsibility for faults rather than blaming people, external forces, or tragedy. In contrast, they are ready to ascribe achievement to their team members, quickly sharing credit and accepting blame when things go wrong.

This particular approach accomplishes two important goals: it empowers team members to take ownership of their actions and develops a sense of collective accountability. As a consequence, team members are free to assume leadership responsibilities without fear of failure, knowing that they are part of a supportive environment where accountability is encouraged and success is shared.

This approach to leadership not only makes people feel good, but it also fosters new ideas and creativity. People on a team are more likely to think outside the box and come up with new ideas when they are recognized and given credit for their work. For the business as a whole, this attitude of open praise and shared responsibility can be constructive. For example, Google has remained at the top of its field, thanks in large part to the way its founders led the company to be constantly open to new ideas. Google is one of the most successful and wealthy companies in the world because it consistently introduces new products and services.

Roy T. Bennett said it well: "*Great leaders make more leaders, not followers.*" This feeling sums up what unusual leadership is all about. Unconventional leaders don't hold on to credit and make people dependent; instead, they have a goal that goes beyond personal gain. They all share this goal, which encourages other people to find their own ways to succeed. In this way, they create a lively setting where people are free to think outside the box and take initiative.

Traditional leaders, on the other hand, tend to take credit for their accomplishments and place the blame on others. When you treat people this way, they may be afraid to express their thoughts or take calculated risks. These traditional leaders may be successful in their own right, but they may struggle to harness the creativity, innovation, and teamwork that unusual leaders can.

To sum up, unusual leaders stand out because they are willing to give credit where credit is due, take responsibility where it is due, and empower their team members. This method not only creates a happy and creative workplace, but it also lays the groundwork for long-term success for the company. Unconventional leaders put the growth and development of their teams ahead of the achievements of individuals. Ultimately, they reap the benefits of a cohesive, inspired, and creative workforce.

III. Defies Conventional Wisdom

Unconventional leaders dare to defy well-documented approaches to peak productivity and traditional leadership frameworks. They understand that there is no one-size-fits-all solution to effective leadership. Instead, they emphasize the need to tailor leadership styles to the unique demands and dynamics of each company and its workforce.

These leaders recognize that a successful approach to leadership necessitates a careful balance. On the one hand, they recognize the need for structure and order in attaining goals. On the other hand, they recognize the importance of creating an environment that stimulates innovation and experimentation. This balanced approach ensures that the team performs effectively while remaining open to new and innovative ideas and solutions.

Unconventional leaders focus on two critical factors: performance and staff morale. They recognize that producing quantifiable results is crucial for success, but they also value the importance of a motivated and engaged workforce. Because of this dual emphasis, they are able to generate not just productivity but also work satisfaction and general well-being among their team members.

Charles R. "Cork" Walgreen III[22] is a stunning example of leadership that prioritizes both performance and employee morale. From 1975 to 2000, he led Walgreens to extraordinary success, surpassing the stock market by a staggering 16-to-1 ratio.

A discussion among Cork Walgreens's senior team over the future of Walgreens' food service business was a watershed point in his leadership experience. With his keen financial

---

[22] **Charles R. "Cork" Walgreen III,** the grandson of Charles Walgreen Sr., founder of the Walgreens drugstore chain in 1901, began his career as a stock boy in 1952. After earning a pharmacy degree from the University of Michigan in 1958, he climbed the ranks to become president in 1969, CEO in 1971, and chairman in 1976. During his tenure, Walgreens doubled the company's store count to over 1,200, shifted its focus to pharmacy, and divested from non-core businesses. He stepped down as CEO in 1998, retired as chairman in 1999, and left the board in 2010. In 2004, he donated $2 million to the University of Michigan College of Pharmacy to endow a professorship on healthcare policy research.

sense, Walgreen saw a watershed moment: the company's best potential was in quick drugstores, not food service.

Making this critical decision, however, took steadfast commitment. While meal service was important to the company's earnings, the main difficulty was emotional rather than financial. Walgreens had a long history, including the creation of the renowned malted milkshake, and food service was firmly ingrained in the family heritage, dating back to Cork's grandfather. In an odd twist, several of the food-service establishments, such as the restaurant chain Corky's, bore the CEO's own name.

Despite this, Cork Walgreen's dedication to the company's long-term prosperity trumped emotion and family history. He saw that for Walgreens to thrive, it needed to rededicate itself to becoming the world's leading provider of convenient drugstores. This meant letting go of any activities that did not align with this strategic goal, regardless of their historical importance.

Cork Walgreen's approach to leadership in this project was characterized by calm persistence and steadfast simplicity. His ability to prioritize the company's performance and strategic direction over sentimental attachments demonstrates the kind of unorthodox leadership that can yield both remarkable achievements and employee well-being.

What genuinely distinguishes unconventional leaders is their willingness to challenge traditional ideas and assumptions. They recognize that upsetting established conventions and practices is often required for innovation. Rather than fearing uncertainty, they embrace it, understanding that not knowing all the answers is a normal part of the road toward advancement. Failure is viewed as a positive learning experience rather than a sign of ineptitude in this workplace.

Unconventional leaders foster an environment in which calculated risks are not only tolerated but encouraged. They believe in creating a safety net for their team members, allowing them to take chances and try new things without fear of being judged harshly. In the words of Leo F. Buscaglia, a well-known American author and motivational speaker, *"Risks must be taken because the greatest hazard in life is to risk nothing."* This idea is embodied by unconventional leaders who recognize that taking calculated risks is an essential element of the innovation process.

Unconventional leaders are distinguished by their bold attitude to challenge conventional thought. They recognize the need for adaptation and a readiness to accept change in order to drive development and innovation. They encourage their team members to push the boundaries of what is possible by cultivating a culture of resilience and innovation, eventually driving both personal and organizational success.

IV. An Observant Listener

Communication expert Frank Luntz used to say, *"It's not what you say; it's what people hear."* To me, that is the crux of emotional communication. Often, we perceive what others are saying factually and logically, yet we remain emotionally disconnected. This can result in our hearing the complete opposite of what others intend to say.

Unconventional leaders understand the power of effective communication, which involves not just imparting information but empowering others to share it further. These leaders prioritize two key qualities: conciseness and candor. Being concise ensures clarity, while being candid means speaking the unvarnished truth, fostering a deep understanding and resonance among team members.

They excel in the art of attentive listening, setting them apart from the conventional. While many managers claim to have an open-door policy, unconventional leaders take it a step further. When engaged in conversation with them, you have their undivided attention. It's as if the world fades away, leaving only you and them at that moment. This level of focus fosters a profound sense of connection and trust between the leader and their team, a hallmark of their exceptional leadership approach.

This continuous commitment to active listening goes beyond courtesy; it fosters an environment where team members feel appreciated and heard. In such an environment, ideas flow freely, and open communication thrives. Unconventional leaders recognize that a workplace where team members truly feel heard fosters innovation and collaboration.

Their approach to listening is a fundamental difference. Unconventional leaders do not simply listen with the intention of responding, as is often the case with traditional leaders. Instead, they listen with the sincere aim of absorbing and comprehending what is being communicated. When someone is really involved in a conversation with you, you can tell. Phones are put aside, and constant eye contact is maintained throughout the engagement.

This seemingly simple act of focused concentration has significant implications. It distinguishes unconventional leaders since they are not focused on drafting their response as you speak. They genuinely engage in the dialogue, exhibiting their dedication to understanding and supporting their team members.

While working on an overseas project, I had the opportunity to collaborate with a project manager from Japan. Despite facing language barriers due to his limited English proficiency, our ability to carry out our ideas remained astonishingly seamless. Interestingly, his limited English skills actually proved to be an advantage as he demonstrated exceptional attentiveness while listening and would diligently repeat my instructions to others in the exact manner I conveyed them.

In the end, it was his focused and systematic approach to listening and communicating that contributed greatly to the success of our project, demonstrating that excellent communication can bridge language gaps and pave the way for smooth collaboration.

A quote by Drishti Bablani, founder of Wordions. *"Listening isn't just about being quiet; it is about using your eyes, ears, and heart to listen to what is spoken, what is unsaid, and what is meant."* Unconventional leaders embody this ideology. They put in time and effort to grasp both the stated and unspoken sides of communication, knowing that genuine comprehension goes beyond words.

Unconventional leaders establish a solid foundation of trust and rapport within their teams by actively and empathetically listening to their team members. They take the time to engage on a personal level, learning about each team member's individual needs and objectives. This in-depth understanding enables them to empower their team by offering the necessary support and assistance to help individuals achieve their goals and succeed.

Unconventional leaders, in essence, utilize the power of attentive listening to cultivate a dynamic and collaborative work environment. They develop solid connections built on trust and mutual respect by giving their entire attention and fully knowing their team members. As a result, their teams thrive, fulfill their full potential, and achieve exceptional success together.

V. Diversifies

In the world of leadership, there is a natural tendency to surround ourselves with people who share our interests and quickly agree with our points of view. In the corporate world, having a workforce that nods in agreement and follows directions quickly may seem comfortable. After all, isn't collaboration necessary for accomplishing common goals? Unconventional leaders, on the other hand, soar beyond the usual by actively pursuing diversity and fostering a range of opinions within their teams.

What distinguishes these leaders is their commitment to questioning the existing quo and deliberately cultivating diversity. They understand the fundamental worth of differences and opposing opinions. Rather than being afraid of opposition, unconventional leaders use it to identify novel solutions. They recognize that when a group approaches challenges from different perspectives, it frequently results in inventive and brilliant solutions—an approach that is becoming increasingly important in today's ever-changing corporate landscape.

Indeed, variety is a pillar of creativity. Thriving organizations require the involvement of people from all backgrounds with a wide range of talents and viewpoints. Malcolm Forbes summed it up perfectly when he said, "*Diversity: the art of thinking independently together.*" Unconventional leaders deliberately foster this variety, understanding that genuine creativity thrives on the harmonic interaction of multiple views and viewpoints.

The risk of becoming trapped in an echo chamber is something that unorthodox leaders are wary of. They recognize that without a chorus of opposing viewpoints, teams may unintentionally restrict their potential. The addition of a second point of view serves as a critical litmus test, helping teams identify potential flaws in their methods and discover more effective paths to achieving shared goals. Furthermore, diverse viewpoints foster new ideas, frequently leading to novel solutions that might otherwise be overlooked. Exposure to diverse perspectives becomes the key to unlocking individual and collective potential, generating new ways of thinking and understanding. Through their joint expertise and variety of perspectives, teams find their way to greater achievement.

These leaders stimulate innovative thinking and more robust solutions by cultivating an atmosphere where opposing ideas are welcomed and appreciated. Predictable environments, comprehensive analysis, and planning enable companies to develop strategies based on position, which leverage the advantages achieved through scale differentiation or capabilities. However, in today's fast-paced corporate environment, embracing diversity is not simply a choice; it is a necessity for long-term sustainability and adaptability.

Home movie and video game rental services giant Blockbuster Video was founded in 1985 and is arguably one of the most iconic brands in the video rental space. During its peak in 2004, Blockbuster employed a significant number of people worldwide and operated thousands of stores.

Unfortunately, due to its inability to adapt to digital advancements, Blockbuster faced financial challenges and ultimately filed for bankruptcy in 2010. In 2000, Netflix approached Blockbuster with an offer to acquire the company for US$50 million.

However, the Blockbuster CEO declined the offer, perceiving it as a "tiny niche business" that was not profitable at that time. Fast forward to July 2017, Netflix had amassed a substantial global subscriber base of 103.95 million and generated a revenue of US$8.8 billion.

The story doesn't simply conclude here! It is worth mentioning that a significant 88 percent of Fortune 500 companies that existed in 1955 have unfortunately ceased to exist, as reported by the American Enterprise Institute. We are all well-acquainted with the downfall of some renowned giants such as KODAK, POLAROID, COMPAQ, GENERAL MOTORS, TOYS R US, PAN AM, BORDERS, and many more. The lesson? Companies that win in the long term prioritize creative disruption, innovation, and future needs.

So, running the company and, at the same time, reinventing it— that's the challenge. This requires continuous experimentation, as planning alone is insufficient under conditions of rapid change and unpredictability. So, while everyone else is busy "saving" the company, unconventional leaders picture the targeted end state and the foundational innovation that will support new growth. Then, once the firm's survival is secure, they communicate the change of direction and gear.

VI. Constant Learner

The traditional leader is seen as the repository of wisdom and knowledge, and their life experiences inform their judgment. We frequently adopt the same strategy because of its familiarity and success. The comfort and satisfaction of doing things the same way every time can also potentially result in time and energy savings. However, this strategy may also lead to a lack of innovation and stagnation. To succeed in a rapidly changing world, we must be receptive to new concepts and alternative approaches.

An unconventional leader is open-minded at all times. Naiveté almost permeates their approach to situations. They are unafraid to make mistakes and are willing to take risks. They are not afraid to challenge the status quo and constantly look for ways to improve the current system. They are driven by a desire to make a difference and are not satisfied with the status quo. While the proof is in the pudding, an unconventional leader is willing to change how things are done. You'll find they acknowledge they don't know everything. But to innovate, humility is required. They are open to feedback and understand the need to adapt. They are humble enough to learn from their mistakes and are willing to set aside their pride for the sake of progress.

An unconventional leader is even willing to get mentored or learn from younger people. After all, a millennial won't understand things the way someone from *Generation Z will.* Roy T Bennett, *the author of "The Light in the Heart," wrote: "Great leaders can see the greatness in others when they can't see it themselves and lead them to their highest potential; they don't even know."*

VII. A Master of Insight

Their ability to maintain an unshakable focus and infinite stamina is undeniably an incredible talent, one that inspires appreciation for its embodiment of discipline, drive, and the necessary components for success in any area. Possessing such an impregnable strength of attention and determination is a priceless advantage on the path to accomplishing one's objectives and unleashing one's full potential. Even the most motivated people, however, have limitations. At this point, the wisdom of taking a break and recharging comes into play, a technique that not only boosts productivity but also reduces burnout while encouraging creativity and insight.

A thorough grasp of personal boundaries is a characteristic of unconventional leadership. Unconventional leaders understand the value of setting limits and the need for rejuvenation in order to return to their positions at their best. This understanding is analogous to a marathon runner training for a race, where pacing oneself and allowing for enough rest are critical to providing top performance on race day. In the context of leadership, this often requires setting aside time to reflect.

Unconventional leaders reflect on their past triumphs and failures during these moments, engaging in a purposeful process of examination and learning. This introspection is a priceless source of growth and development, allowing people to re-evaluate their progress, fine-tune their plans, and recalibrate their goals. It's a talent that may not get the recognition it deserves, but unconventional leaders are not only familiar with it but also highly skilled in its use.

A shining illustration of this attribute can be found in the leadership of Smith, who played a pivotal role in the remarkable transformation of Kimberly-Clark. Smith's tenacious determination became particularly evident when he faced what would become the most dramatic decision in the company's history: the decision to sell its mills.

To provide some background, Smith and his team reached a serious conclusion about the company's primary business—coated paper—shortly after he took over as CEO. They knew it would struggle to make money and that it faced little competition. They did, however, see a chance. They believed that by entering the highly competitive consumer paper goods market, where profits were higher, and giants like Procter & Gamble were already present, Kimberly-Clark would have to perform well or face bankruptcy.

Smith made a significant announcement, drawing on the famous military strategy of setting fire to one's own boats as soon as they land on enemy territory. This leaves no way to escape and forces troops to either succeed or die. Kimberly-Clark would sell its mills, including the ones in Kimberly, Wisconsin, that gave the company its name. All the money generated from this vast choice would be reinvested in the consumer business and strategically allocated to brands like Huggies diapers and Kleenex tissues.

Business media were skeptical of Smith's bold move, and Wall Street experts lowered the stock price of the company. Despite uncertainty and pressure from external sources, Smith remained true to his goal. After 25 years, Kimberly-Clark not only acquired Scott Paper but also outperformed Procter & Gamble in six out of eight product groups. Smith looked back on his remarkable journey with a breathtakingly simple statement: "*I never stopped trying to become qualified for the job.*" This sentence encapsulates his unwavering dedication to improvement and growth, making him a great example of innovative leadership.

VIII. Unafraid of Unpopular Stances

Standing out and holding controversial opinions can be intimidating, as most individuals try to avoid sticking out like a sore thumb. This proclivity can unintentionally lead to groupthink, a phenomenon in which group members tend to adopt the majority opinion, even if it is erroneous. Accepting controversial viewpoints, on the other hand, serves a vital role in encouraging independent thinking and questioning the status quo, which is a necessary stimulant for advancement in any profession. The fear of being judged or not being taken seriously by peers and superiors often silences dissident voices, resulting in a conformist environment that stifles creativity and innovation. This quiet is widespread at many workplaces, despite executive ideas conflicting with the company's ideals.

Unconventional leaders, on the other hand, distinguish themselves by upholding inspired standards. They foster a culture of trust and respect in which employees are not just allowed but encouraged to express their views and opinions. In reality, unconventional leaders strongly encourage employees to submit feedback, participate in debates, and contribute to the decision-making processes of the firm. The connection between these leaders and their team members is like tending to a plant, requiring regular maintenance and attention. The CEO provides fertile soil, nutritious water, and necessary sunlight, while the workers contribute the ideas and energy that drive the organization's development and success.

These leaders are frequently distinguished by their determination to remain steady in the face of resistance. They are adamant about their ideals, which they see as crucial to the company's success. "*Be the change you want to see in the world,*" Mahatma Gandhi said. This statement highlights their unshakeable dedication to their beliefs, even if it means swimming against the current.

Taking on controversial viewpoints requires a high level of guts and fortitude. It requires standing firm when arguing for an alternative viewpoint to popular thinking. Unconventional leaders recognize that it is precisely these controversial positions that may lead to game-changing innovation and revolution. Their unshakable devotion to their ideals and openness to opposing viewpoints create a climate where innovative ideas may thrive, and the company can progress.

Let's take the example of George Cain's tenure as CEO of Abbott Laboratories, which serves as a compelling illustration of a leader who fearlessly embraced unpopular decisions in the pursuit of excellence.

When Cain assumed the helm of Abbott Laboratories, the company faced a challenging situation. It was a family-controlled business, languishing at the lower echelons of the pharmaceutical industry, heavily reliant on its cash cow, erythromycin. Unlike charismatic leaders who inspire through their personalities, Cain's strength lay in his unyielding commitment to excellence. He harbored an intense aversion to mediocrity, refusing to accept "good enough" in any form. Over the course of the next 14 years, he unwaveringly imposed his vision for greatness upon Abbott Labs.

One of Cain's initial and bold steps was addressing a systemic issue plaguing the company: nepotism. With a methodical and unapologetic approach, he meticulously rebuilt both the board and the executive team, appointing only the most qualified individuals he could find. Cain sent a clear message: familial connections would no longer hold sway. If an executive couldn't rise to become the industry's top performer within their sphere of responsibility, they would face the risk of losing their paycheck.

Such a rigorous restructuring might be expected from an outsider brought in to revive a struggling organization. However, what made Cain's actions truly unconventional was his status as an 18-year insider and, even as part of the Abbott family, being the son of a former company president. Though family gatherings in the Cain household may have been tense for a time - "Sorry, I had to let you go. Would you like more turkey?" - Ultimately, family members found solace in the remarkable performance of their stocks. Cain had ignited a growth engine that proved highly profitable. From 1974 to 2000, Abbott delivered shareholder returns that outperformed the market by a factor of 4.5 to 1, surpassing industry titans like Merck and Pfizer.

Leadership is not a popularity contest. If anything, it might be the opposite. In the words of Mahatma Gandhi, "First they ignore you, then they laugh at you, then they fight you, then you win." Staying on the course in the face of resistance, unpopularity, and loneliness requires tremendous inner strength. This strength is the fuel that keeps real leaders from giving up: Leadership Energy, which stems from a sense of purpose and value. Only a few are able to tap into this inherent energy to prevail in the game of creating a better future. George Cain's unwavering commitment to excellence, even when it meant making unpopular decisions within the family, exemplifies the essence of unconventional leadership, marked by fearlessness in the pursuit of greatness.

IX. Integrity

Bill Gates once shared an unconventional approach to hiring, mentioning his preference for engineers who might be considered "lazy" because they find more efficient ways to work. However, the business world often presents temptations to cut corners in the name of cost-saving measures. Unconventional leaders, in contrast, are known for their unwavering honesty, especially when they have autonomy.

Integrity is the core, core value; it's about matching your intent with the content, and it's an expression of your character and credibility. The value of trustworthiness is palpable in the workplace. When you are seen as trustworthy, your superiors are more confident in entrusting you with increased responsibilities, and your team is more inclined to share their challenges and concerns. This trustworthiness is grounded in the understanding that unconventional leaders are accountable not just to a single entity but to several stakeholders, including customers, staff who invest time and energy in the business's growth, and senior management.

Being honest is a challenging task, as people often lie to avoid the difficulties and consequences associated with facing challenges. Individuals and organizations must be receptive to challenges if their perspectives on reality are open to public scrutiny. This requires a constant and ongoing effort to monitor ourselves and ensure that our communications, including not just the words we use but also our tone and manner, accurately reflect the truth or reality to the best of our ability.

The journey that a successful executive must navigate between perseverance and the potential loss of their identity and integrity is incredibly narrow; only a very small number of individuals are able to make this journey successfully. It presents a significant challenge. In the world of business or politics, it is sometimes necessary to withhold one's opinions selectively. If individuals were always to speak their minds, they would be perceived as insubordinate and a threat to the organization by management. They would develop a reputation for being abrasive and would not be trusted to represent the organization. It is inevitable that, in order to be effective within an organization, one must partially conform to its expectations. Therefore, the expression of opinions, feelings, ideas, and even knowledge must be suppressed in certain situations. However, it is essential to consider the guidelines for withholding the truth while upholding integrity.

But most importantly, it is crucial never to tell falsehoods. Withholding the truth can potentially be seen as a form of lying, so each situation requires a moral decision. Personal needs or desires should never be the basis for making these decisions. Decisions should be entirely based on the needs of the person or people from whom the truth is being withheld. This assessment carries a great deal of responsibility and can only be carried out with genuine care and concern for them.

X. Supporting and Building Others

While caring for one's team might be perceived as meekness, it embodies the essence of humility, as described by Jim Collins in his renowned book, "Good to Great." This quality distinguishes the Level of leaders. Unconventional leaders understand that motivating their team requires developing the individual potential of each team member. They believe it will do no harm to review once more the contradictions that caused confusion during previous inquiries. This involves actively challenging one's own opinions and assuming the role of devil's advocate, even when in agreement. Such actions provide a fresh perspective that might otherwise remain unexplored.

For them, leadership can be compared to the act of lovemaking, wherein effectiveness and fulfillment can be achieved by taking one's time, considering the perspectives of others, showing respect throughout the process, embracing natural progression, avoiding competition, and refraining from attempting to exert control or dominance. These leaders act as a working funnel rather than a tunnel. In other words, a great leader does not pass on every request to their team like a mindless forward button.

Instead, they act as a filter, pushing back on unnecessary or unrealistic demands and prioritizing the time and resources of their team.

An unusual trait among unconventional leaders is their genuine desire to cultivate successors. Instead of advocating for equality, they promote the idea of equity! Equity is a more holistic approach to achieving equality, as it considers the specific needs of individuals and communities. Equity takes into account the different backgrounds and experiences of individuals and strives to create a level playing field for everyone. Sets standards of building an enduring great company; will settle for nothing less. They actively engage in building the next generation of leaders, with the intention of passing the torch to those who will continue to advance the company while upholding its core values.

As the late Lee Iacocca, former CEO of Chevrolet until 1992, aptly stated, "*Management is nothing more than motivating other people.*" This stands in contrast to conventional leadership models, which often suggest that teams primarily support their leaders as the more valuable assets.

XI. Invisible

One fantastic thing about unconventional leaders is that they are inherently humble. They focus their attention on outside factors and often give too much credit to those factors. When they can't think of a specific person or event to attribute their success to, they say that success is due to luck or good timing. It's clear that these leaders consistently demonstrate compelling modesty, shun the spotlight, and refrain from bragging about their achievements.

This type of leadership contradicts the opinions of the majority of individuals. People generally think that moving companies from good to great requires charismatic, larger-than-life leaders—people with strong personalities, such as Iacocca, Dunlap, Welch, and Gault—who make headlines and become famous.

Darwin Smith, on the other hand, might have looked like he was from another world. He was shy, humble, and even a little awkward, and he tried to avoid the spotlight. When a reporter asked how he managed his team, Smith answered with a long, unblinking stare from behind his thick, black-rimmed glasses. He looked like a country boy in his first suit, dressed in a simple and somewhat old-fashioned manner. There was a long, awkward pause before he finally said: "Eccentric." As expected, the Wall Street Journal did not write a fascinating article about Darwin Smith.

However, anyone who thought Smith was soft or meek would have been very wrong. His lack of pretense went hand in hand with a firm and stoic desire to live. Smith grew up on a farm in Indiana, where he worked the day shift at International Harvester to pay for night school fees at Indiana University. Unfortunately, Smith lost a finger in a work accident, but he still went back to his evening classes that same day and to work the next morning. This determination ultimately helped the poor but determined Indiana farm boy gain admission to Harvard Law School.

When Smith took over as CEO of Kimberly-Clark, he showed the same strong will. As a strange turn of events, doctors told him he had nose and throat cancer just two months into his job as CEO, giving him less than a year to live. Smith didn't give up. He informed the board immediately that he was ill and made it clear that he wouldn't be giving up anytime soon. Smith maintained his busy work schedule while traveling from Wisconsin to Houston once a week for radiation treatment. It's hard to believe he lived another 25 years. Of those, 20 were spent running Kimberly-Clark.

The ability to put others before oneself is a trait of unconventional leaders. Great leaders often find themselves in the spotlight because their extroverted personalities are essential to the success of their teams or companies. But being unorthodox doesn't mean you only do things in a novel way. Many of the unsung heroes who have taken their companies from the depths of despair to the heights of success have been driven by ambition but have put the needs of others ahead of their own. The question in today's corporate world is whether or not we have the courage to accept humility when things get tough.

Take a moment to reflect on a leader who may have caused you frustration or disappointment. Consider the extent to which they exhibited the tendencies mentioned earlier and how many of the characteristics listed apply to them. It is possible that your negative experiences with leadership were a result of leaders who followed conventional norms rather than those who forged their own character. Now, think about the leader you admire the most. It is likely that this person exhibited more unconventional character traits instead of conforming to traditional leadership tendencies. The importance of character extends beyond personal preference; it has practical implications. As leaders, we lead based on our own values and beliefs, and these qualities shape who we are. The more power or influence we have, the more our true selves are amplified. That is why leaders must prioritize the development of their character. Others rely on it.

The underlying insight is that leadership, in essence, can be seen as a service that people in an organization "buy" or "don't buy." Leaders have customers in the sense that they serve two key constituencies: their bosses, who expect them to deliver results, and their followers, who rely on them for guidance and support. In effect, people buy your leadership when they value your leadership practices. As a result, they are inspired to excel and act with commitment. Employees who don't buy into your leadership style tend to disengage, becoming non-customers. Analyzing unconventional leadership in this way allows us to see how the frameworks and concepts of quantum leadership that we are discussing can also assist leaders in re-engaging disengaged employees.

Quantum Leadership is not just a departure from tradition but a transformative shift in how we envision leadership itself. It is an approach that values authenticity, innovation, trust, and humility. Quantum Leaders serve as beacons of inspiration in a world that demands constant adaptation and agility, blazing the route towards a more inclusive, innovative, and impactful future. Quantum Leadership invites us to embrace change, challenge norms, and lead with unflinching integrity and absolute dedication to the growth and well-being of all those we have the pleasure of leading as we navigate the complexities of the current business world.

***

CHAPTER-3
Leadership Reimagined

- **A Framework**

As part of "Leadership Reimagined," let's take a journey to discover new, innovative approaches to leadership with Spiritual Quotient (SQ) that go beyond the status quo.

The SQ method is all about delving deep into our inner selves to find solutions to significant issues that often go undetected in our hectic lives. Reflection, introspection, and self-awareness are our trusted companions on our road of self-discovery. The heart of this method remains the same: to assist individuals in understanding their purpose, what motivates it, and what influences their decision-making.

The SQ method equips participants with the skills to explore the depths of their own souls as they pursue personal growth and self-discovery. It is a journey in which they grow to better understand themselves, not only on the surface but at their heart. The emphasis is on discovering one's own strengths and limitations, unwinding the threads of one's values, and perfecting the skill of making decisions based on one's own unique sense of purpose. The core message is clear: the SQ method empowers individuals to live more meaningful lives.

The notion of Spiritual Quotient, or SQ, is at the center of it all, a measure that assesses a person's ability to function from a state of being rather than simple knowing or doing.

It's about being genuine, compassionate, and distant at the same time. The core concept remains the same: SQ assesses the depth of one's connection with oneself and the environment around them.

Consider SQ to be a compass, leading us through the perilous maze of life. We become more authentic when we act from a sense of Being. We stop pretending to be someone we're not and start being ourselves. This concept's simplicity stays intact— it's about being authentic, honest, and genuine to oneself.

Empathy, another pillar of SQ, is our ability to connect deeply with others. It is not enough to utter the proper words; it is also necessary to fully comprehend what people are going through and to provide steadfast support. The nature of empathy, which is central to the SQ method, remains unchanged.

The third piece of the SQ jigsaw is detachment, which involves maintaining a healthy distance from life's ups and downs. It does not imply that we become indifferent or detached; instead, it permits us to negotiate life's obstacles without becoming overwhelmed.

This notion is as simple as it has always been: **Achieving balance in our emotional responses.**

Journey to Spiritual Leadership
Spiritual Leadership
Lead authentically, inspire genuinely.
5
Detachment
Maintain emotional balance in life
4
3
Empathy
Connecting deeply with others' experiences
2
Authenticity
Being Genuine and true to oneself
1
Self-Reflection
Exploring inner self for solutions

- **Unlock the Potential of Spiritual Quotient (SQ) in Leadership "Seven-ways"**

In the world of leadership, there's an invaluable yet often overlooked tool—the Spiritual Quotient (SQ). To understand how SQ can elevate leadership, let's explore its fundamental principles and how they can transform your approach:

I. Establish a Presence

Building a personal brand is similar to creating your own distinct personality, based on your unique DNA, beyond the constraints of your profession or organization. It's about reclaiming control of your professional image and revealing your actual self to the world. Throughout this trip, you must resist allowing others to define who you are and instead take control over how you are perceived.

Occupying the Chair represents a position of influence or authority based on your position rather than your personal brand. It is similar to the trails left behind by a soaring plane, which are separate from the plane itself. You may have witnessed these trails in the sky, lasting for hours after the plane has passed, but they do not define the plane itself. With a single gust of wind, the twin smoke plumes disperse, and the condensed atmosphere simply dissolves.

Your personal brand is an expression of your character and actions, which have already been established and may not be easily altered. It is similar to throwing a ball— once released, it follows a predetermined trajectory and cannot be halted. It continues on its course and will eventually reach its destination. This behavior is automatic and consistent.

If you genuinely desire to succeed with all your heart and your determination is volcanic and explosive, waiting to erupt with massive energy, then please consider this: check your addictions. Specifically, your passive habits. It's common for all of us to have them, as humans are creatures of habit. And that's perfectly fine. In fact, this reality can be harnessed to work in our favor and contribute significantly to our follow-through behavior. The question is: Are your addictions positive or negative? Perhaps a mix, you might say. Of course! So, let's go to work to clean up your act! Take a look at your eating habits, relaxation habits, reading habits, exercise habits, and sexual habits. Would it be fair to say that no one really needs to lecture you? We are all capable of discerning right from wrong without needing external criticism. It may be beneficial to focus on the potential benefits of positive habits while being cautious of harmful addictions that could potentially harm you.

If there is anything you need to understand, it is necessary to remove certain aspects, such as pride, anger, bitterness, pain, jealousy, and self-pity. For example, on my birthday, I received a book that was beautifully wrapped as a gift. However, I cannot simply keep it in the gift packaging and admire it on my bookshelf. I must unwrap the gift. Although I sometimes prefer the gift wrap paper over the book itself, it is the book that is the true gift, not the paper. Therefore, I carefully removed the paper. Now, I need to open the book and read it. By progressing from the outer layers to the innermost, we can uncover our true essence.

Your authentic image lies in your graceful departure rather than your grand entrance. Out! Fired! Divorced! Separated? Parting ways? Departing! Death? Bankruptcy? Lost your lease? Unexpected changes in the market? All of us are going out—sometime, someway, somewhere! When you go from success to failure, failure to success, health to sickness, and life to death, what kind of attitude will you have? How you exit is of utmost importance, as it will impact your reputation and determine whether you will enjoy the remainder of your journey.

"The Rock," Dwayne Johnson, has a formula for success that he's ready to share: "I'm always asked, 'What's the secret to success?' "However, there are no secrets. Be modest. You should be hungry. And always be the hardest-working person in the room."

In essence, don't try to imitate; instead, know your personal brand and stay true to it. It's like creating your own formula for success, one that's tailored to your own interests and abilities. Consider it a secret sauce that helps you stand out. While you may modify the components as you go, it's essential to adhere to your original recipe. Be yourself, be genuine, and most importantly, have fun with the process.

II. Turn a Potential Foe into an Ally

The ability to transform a prospective opponent into a trusted friend is a valuable talent in the realms of leadership and cooperation. It is a process based on transparency, compromise, and a thorough knowledge of the needs and viewpoints of others.

Begin by addressing your internal conflicts, which arise when your values come into conflict. It is essential to consider the impact your actions may have on others, even if you are driven to progress. Therefore, it is essential to establish a firm and reliable framework of moral and ethical principles. Adhere to these principles diligently and proceed with confidence towards your goals.

It's imperative to harmonize with your inner conflicts and address inevitable contradictions; otherwise, you will lack enthusiasm and drive to succeed. Vapid, wavering leadership will emerge, spelling "failure waiting to happen." Be harsh on yourself. You can't run with the hares and dash with the hounds. Your leadership style must have moral fiber. Say "yes" to what is right and "no" to what is wrong. And you will find peace in your heart! Once you have achieved this, you will be better equipped to handle any external conflicts that may arise.

Conflict is an inevitable part of achieving success; therefore, do not deceive yourself. Every time you do anything significant, people criticize you or find fault. As a human being, you are not perfect. Negative aspects are inherent in every project. Each time you set a new goal, you can expect a new set of tensions. All good ideas are flawed in some way. Make sure you are prepared for conflict.

To effectively manage conflicts, it is crucial to anticipate their occurrence and identify the possible individuals and situations involved. Before acting, gather a group of knowledgeable and reliable individuals to discuss strategies for preventing conflicts. Conflict prevention is often more effective than conflict resolution.

If conflict is inevitable, it is important to address and resolve it. The initial approach should involve attempting to reconcile with the individuals involved. Treat them respectfully, and do not underestimate their worth.

People who belittle people will be little people and accomplish little!

The initial step is to embrace an open-minded approach and a mindset of unity. It is necessary to be receptive to contrary opinions and encourage those with reservations to share their thoughts and concerns. Politely inquire, "Do you have any reservations you want to express?" "Constructive conversations help us resolve, so please let us know if your concerns have been addressed and if you are ready to support our decision. If not, we can hold off and use the time before the next meeting to find a mutually acceptable compromise. It is crucial that everyone be wholeheartedly involved in this project."

It is essential to keep in mind that individuals who make demands may face resistance, those who feel defeated may encounter indifference, and those who are dedicated will receive assistance.

It is worth acknowledging the merits of your opposition, even if they may be mistaken, as they might have some valid points. Take the time to listen and learn from them. It is advisable to address any issues openly and comprehensively in a private setting rather than disregarding the points of tension and facing the consequences later on.

In essence, converting a potential opponent into an ally is cultivating an environment of trust and understanding. In the long run, this foundation can lead to more robust and more productive partnerships. Just as animals in the wild rely on collaboration to thrive, people benefit from mutual respect and a willingness to compromise in any collaborative endeavor.

So, whether you're navigating workplace dynamics or forming alliances, keep in mind the power of converting prospective adversaries into allies. Building bridges and forming a unified front for shared success requires openness, compromise, and empathy.

III. Forgiveness is the Key

Forgiveness is a fundamental thread in the fabric of life, weaving a calm and harmonious existence together. Indeed, it is the key to living a life filled with peace and compassion. Forgiveness has a profound impact when it enables us to release grudges, anger, and resentment, allowing us to move forward with a heart filled with understanding and empathy.

Forgiveness acts as a bridge between our past and present. It enables us to make amends for past deeds and mistakes while also promising a brighter future. In this sense, forgiving becomes a self-care act, a balm that soothes our inner unrest and leads us to inner peace.

This virtue is more than a footnote in life; it is a fundamental component of our human experience. It shifts our attention from concentrating on the past to appreciating the current moment. We accept responsibility for our own acts when we forgive, allowing us to make peace with ourselves. It is a self-love and self-respecting act, an assertion that we are worthy of grace and understanding.

At its root, forgiveness is a sort of healing. It is a catalyst for better relationships, emotional well-being, and, eventually, a more fulfilling existence. It directs us towards the light, illuminating the route to a spiritual existence, like a beacon in the darkness.

Throughout history, famous people have demonstrated the transformative power of forgiveness. One such example is

Pope John Paul II's forgiveness of his would-be murderer[23], overcoming animosity to embrace compassion and reconciliation. Rep. John Lewis's forgiveness of George Wallace is another poignant example of how forgiveness can break down walls of hate and prejudice. According to Paul Bradley Smith, "Forgiveness is brave; it sets us free from darkness, and it allows light to shine the sweet fragrance of life into our souls." These lines reflect the essence of forgiveness, portraying it as a brave act that frees us from the bonds of negativity, enabling the dazzling light of a more purposeful existence to pervade our own souls.

Accepting forgiveness allows us to see the world with fresh eyes, filled with compassion and a heart overflowing with the beautiful aroma of a life well-lived. In the enormous tapestry of life, forgiveness is a brilliant and transformational color, from guilt to pardon, from condemnation to forgiveness, that enriches the fabric of our being.

IV. Ally with Powerful People or Organizations

The saying "A problem shared is a problem halved" applies to business just as it does to other areas of life. Building a long-term alliance with a prominent individual or organization with whom you can collaborate, exchange ideas, and rely on during tough times can be game-changing in leadership and cooperation. It's a journey built on trust, respect, and strategic preparation, analogous to

[23] On 13 May 1981, **Pope John Paul II** was shot in St. Peter's Square by Mehmet Ali Ağca, suffering severe blood loss. Ağca was quickly apprehended and sentenced to life in prison. The Pope forgave him and requested his pardon from Italian president Carlo Azeglio Ciampi, leading to Ağca's deportation to Turkey in June 2000. He converted to Roman Catholicism in 2007.

building a solid bridge between two formidable entities. A well-thought-out architectural plan secures the stability of the bridge, just as a well-designed cooperation strategy sets the route for a successful partnership.

A thorough examination of successful individuals and organizations reveals a network, whether obvious or subtle, that contributes to their success. The importance of foreign policies is widely recognized, as evidenced by the adverse outcomes that result from poor policies. Sometimes, it becomes more crucial to consider "who you know?" rather than "what you know." You may be a highly skilled eye specialist, but when your hospital requires cardiac surgery, it is vital to seek out a heart surgeon. Our bodies are intricately interconnected with a network of blood vessels, ranging from major arteries to tiny capillaries that nourish every living cell. Similarly, a network of nerves extends from the brain to every tissue, enabling the transmission of messages throughout the body. Without this remarkable network, the powerful heart or the brilliant mind would struggle to maintain control and achieve success.

Allies differ from stakeholders, who are individuals with an interest in the work you do and who have the potential to help or hinder it. Relationships with stakeholders tend to be more functional than with your allies. Additionally, allies should not be confused with coaches and mentors, as their primary goal is to support your skill development and growth. Nonetheless, it is worth noting that coaches, mentors, and stakeholders can also serve as allies.

It may take some time to identify the individuals you wish to collaborate with—individuals who are also interested in allying with you, even if you are aware of where to search. Hence, it is crucial to prioritize building strong and valuable relationships. When you come across people at conferences, work settings, or even on social media platforms, you are essentially establishing contacts. However, it is essential to note that merely making contacts may not always lead to a genuine connection.

High-quality connections are interactions that can make individuals feel engaged, open, motivated, and revitalized. These connections are not solely reliant on close or intimate relationships; even a brief message or a simple exchange during a meeting can be considered of high quality if it leaves both participants feeling valued and appreciated. When your connections are of high quality, they have the potential to transform a conversation into one that benefits everyone involved.

"Friendship is not by force, but by choice," wrote Stella Oladiran, a Nigerian novelist.

It is difficult to satisfy everyone's preferences; those who attempt to do so ultimately fail to satisfy anyone. Striving to fulfill every desire or expectation is a recipe for disappointment. Here are some suggestions to consider for establishing long-lasting alliances.

- **Be supportive**

Support potential allies or talented individuals when you observe that they require assistance. If you are still determining their specific needs, consider asking them. Your openness, support, and positivity will increase their willingness to lend you theirs.

❖ **Nurture the relationship**

One good deed or a single act of kindness won't be enough to form an alliance. To build and maintain strong connections, you must regularly engage and interact with both potential and current allies.

❖ **Communication**

Effective and timely communication is crucial for the growth of any relationship, especially when differences or competing loyalties are involved.

❖ **Be reasonable**

Be realistic in understanding the level of support expected; it is essential to acknowledge that it may not always be available. Despite their willingness and best efforts, their own responsibilities and priorities may sometimes take precedence over yours.

❖ **Don't be offended**

You or your allies may need to say "No" to one another occasionally, but remember the trust you have built together. To avoid "burning bridges," don't retaliate or withhold support. Instead, seek help from other sources or negotiate a compromise.

It is crucial to develop a comprehensive plan for collaboration and communication before embarking on this trip. This plan serves as a blueprint, outlining the duties, responsibilities, and objectives of each party.

One of the most well-known instances of a strategic alliance is the partnership between Starbucks and Target. You may have come across this example of a strategic alliance frequently. When you enter Target, you will find a

Starbucks counter ready to prepare your preferred beverage. Target and Starbucks understand that their brands have a similar audience: busy shoppers seeking affordable "luxuries" and a quick break. This strategic alliance was established all the way back in 1999 and continues to thrive. Numerous Target stores now feature Starbucks cafes, offering a convenient way for customers to rejuvenate during their shopping trips. Target customers can be assured that if they feel hungry or thirsty while shopping, Starbucks is readily accessible right within the store.

Starbucks has formed a fruitful in-store collaboration with Barnes & Noble, showcasing its ability to thrive despite the formidable presence of Amazon. A contributing factor to their ongoing success is the presence of the co-branded Starbucks “B&N Cafes” within numerous Barnes & Noble outlets. This delightful combination of a refreshing beverage and an engaging book has consistently offered book lovers an added incentive to visit a physical Barnes & Noble store rather than resorting to online purchases or exploring alternative competitors.

Trust and respect are the bedrock of every sustainable partnership. These aspects, like the bricks and mortar of a bridge, offer the structural stability upon which the alliance is based. Without confidence, an alliance is like a shaky bridge that would collapse under the weight of obstacles.

V. Be an Active Team Player

If you are interested in donning leadership gloves, then goalkeeping is an excellent example of experiential learning. When a goal goes in, everyone looks at you. Do you have what it takes to deal with that?

Having a strong mentality is crucial in this role, as you are often subjected to criticism. Leaders don't get paid every month because they're good. They get paid so they can remain resilient in the face of criticism and spread the positive influence of leadership among the people, reflected through their contagious smiles. Similar to a goalkeeper, you are the final line of defense. How do you cope when you make a mistake? It is essential to recover positively and show resilience. While it may seem harsh, maintaining the right attitude can overcome disappointment and demonstrate reliability to the team.

Frequently, A goalkeeper is left embarrassed following a mistake, and the most mature way of handling it is to assume responsibility for it and never allow it to distract from performance thereafter. When we are directly responsible for a mistake, it is futile to point fingers; instead, we should focus on fixing the resulting damage. "For leaders, there is no hiding place." A good leader takes responsibility for failures and shares in the accolades. We are not perfect and make mistakes occasionally. True leaders use these experiences as opportunities to learn and improve, addressing any issues before they recur.

A goalkeeper has the largest vision area in front of him. He can see the formation of both teams ahead and is usually one of the earliest to spot a dangerous attack. Just like a business leader who has a broader view of their business and its many moving parts, they both have the luxury of being removed from 95% of the skirmishes that happen in the normal course of a game or business day. The onus is then on them to communicate with their teammates about their surroundings in the most effective manner. A good leader is vocal. As a leader, you need to be skilled at organizing and motivating your team. You need to see what's going on and respond to the threats!

To achieve a common goal, teammates need to collaborate on the field. Therefore, wise leaders opt to recruit talented individuals who can enhance the team and bring unique skills and expertise. To foster a positive company culture, it is recommended to communicate your vision, values, and mission to both employees and potential candidates. This will ensure that your team consists of like-minded individuals who will work together harmoniously to make progress.

It's crucial to maintain a tight grip on your business and thoroughly understand every aspect of running it. When you have a hand in every aspect of your organization, you hold the critical information necessary to maximize opportunities when a "free kick" comes your way. It's also smart to maintain a steady grasp of customer needs through regular communication that keeps your finger on the market pulse. Being hands-on enables you to take the lead in moving your business forward.

In many games, even a rock-solid defense will experience momentary lapses in concentration. During these moments, a goalkeeper may face an opponent one-on-one, and they may feel helpless in that situation. However, exceptional goalkeepers don't wait for the attacker to gain an advantage; instead, they quickly move forward to reduce the attacker's options for a shot. Similarly, leaders who are highly dependable in vulnerable situations can instill confidence in their team to handle tumultuous situations.

It takes a special breed to dive headfirst at an opponent's foot mid-shot or reach for a cross coming across the goal mouth unprotected, knowing you'll get clobbered. However, sometimes, in the course of a game or business, it is necessary to take calculated risks and prioritize the team's success, even if it means sacrificing personal safety, especially when the stakes are high and the outcome is uncertain. This doesn't mean being reckless is prudent, but with proper training and preparation, one can determine when to take risks and when to be cautious. And sometimes, it's necessary to have faith and be a little unconventional or even a little crazy.

I am fond of Ted Lasso's quote, which states, "*Goldfish are considered the happiest animals because of their short memories.*" Exceptional athletes and successful business leaders prioritize focusing on the present moment rather than dwelling on the past. They prepare themselves for what lies ahead and ensure they have the right mindset to perform their duties. Although the ultimate objective is victory, the journey towards it is also enjoyable. When you have a genuine passion for what you do, like the footballers competing on the World Cup stage, working long hours will not diminish your enthusiasm because you are pursuing your dream. However, it is essential to remember that you are not alone on the field. It is crucial to show respect towards your opponents, the league, and your supporters, as they all contribute to making your efforts worthwhile. When you achieve success, celebrate with your teammates, and then strive to push yourself even further towards the next goal.

Being an active part of your team is like the motor that propels a well-oiled machine in the complicated realm of cooperation and collaboration. Their contributions serve as the gears that propel the team's problem-solving and inventiveness.

Valuing Each Team Member: They understand the significance of each team member's contribution. Each member is a key cog in the machine, and the failure of one element can have a ripple effect on the entire operation.

VI. Have Faith in Yourself

Believing in oneself is the linchpin of personal and professional achievement. It serves as the driving force behind conquering challenges and reaching one's goals. When you possess unwavering self-belief, you hold the power to shape your destiny and overcome obstacles that may come your way.

Self-doubt limits possibilities, while faith reveals opportunities. Non-believers often live cynically, defensively, and fearfully.

Anybody can dream! Anybody can plan! As it says in the Song, "When You Wish Star, it makes no difference who you are." There are no great people, only ordinary people! We are being transformed, carved, and molded by dreams into greatness. Some simply have bigger dreams than others!

So, when you choose to dream, the dream will decide your destiny. The size of the dream will decide how big a person you will become. Then, the dream continues to grow, and the curtain opens to reveal a vision of tomorrow. The dreamer learns that the great dreams of great dreamers are never fulfilled— they are transcended! Hence, they tend to propagate themselves.

The universe searches for the right mind to whom it can entrust the most incredible gift it can give a human being—A dream! The almighty must find someone who will instinctively, intuitively, impulsively, passionately welcome the awesome, impossible idea into his finite human mind as something precious! A fresh love, a newborn child! The universe won't drop the seed on the hard ground of a mind infected with cynicism.

Divine dreams are delegated to dedicated doers! The Almighty grants sacred visions to those individuals who exhibit unwavering faith and wholeheartedly commit themselves to their realization.

Having faith in oneself involves taking a leap into the unknown, making oneself more receptive to new opportunities, and trusting in one's abilities even when there's no concrete evidence to guarantee success. It's the recognition that growth and progress often lie outside the comfort zone. This faith propels you to step into unfamiliar territory. It instills the courage to confront challenges head-on, fully aware that it is within those uncharted waters that the greatest discoveries are made.

Once you let go of your defensive fear and open yourself to receptive love, Setbacks become opportunities for growth, and mistakes transform into valuable lessons. This resilience in the face of adversity enables you to rebound from failures with renewed determination, continually moving forward toward your objectives.

In the eloquent words of Terry Tempest Williams, "*Faith is not about finding meaning in the world; there may be no such thing – faith is the belief in our capacity to create meaningful lives.*" Believing in oneself is not about seeking external validation or meaning; it's about recognizing the boundless potential within and the capacity to shape a life that is both purposeful and meaningful.

The Shaolin monks of China often showcase incredible displays of human strength, such as breaking steel bars with their heads or effortlessly splitting stones with their bare hands. Try searching YouTube for Shaolin Monks or Shaolin Kung Fu if you haven't seen them in action. Once you observe their remarkable skills, you might wonder if their abilities stem from physical or mental strength. I don’t know the exact answer myself, but the power of focusing the mind seems to have a lot to do with their abilities.

VII. Compromise Without Compromising Values

Occasionally, in order to prevent or address conflicts that could potentially have a detrimental impact on your company, we choose to embrace compromise. This approach, referred to as reconciliation, aims to find a mutually agreeable resolution to a dispute. It’s known as a lose-lose strategy since both parties willingly forfeit some of their needs in the interest of reaching an agreement. This can be a quick way to resolve a conflict before it escalates. A compromise can also be used as a temporary measure to avoid conflict until the parties involved can implement a more lasting or permanent solution.

The term "compromise" derives from the Latin phrase "compromissum," which combines the prefix "com-," meaning "together," and the root "promissum," meaning "promise." Like a happy marriage, a healthy professional relationship is built on mutual respect and a shared commitment to working together to achieve a common objective.

The issue at hand is the potential for discussions to escalate into conflicts among individuals, which ultimately hinders productivity. When the necessary amount of friction for movement and progress becomes excessive, it becomes impossible to achieve anything. It is crucial that we find a solution to this problem, as it will otherwise result in stagnation and a lack of progress. In order to mitigate friction, we can employ the ingenious concept of lubrication. By introducing a lubricant, such as oil or grease, between two objects in close contact, we can eliminate friction. This is achieved by introducing a third element. And what is this third element? Fundamentally, it is our shared purpose: collaborating towards the same goal and with the same intentions.

Be open to new ideas and eager to establish common ground via compromise. Take the time, just like a great diplomat, to thoroughly comprehend the other person's needs and interests. You demonstrate respect and understanding for their point of view, creating groundwork for a pleasant working relationship. However, it's a delicate balance that requires self-awareness and assertiveness and must be navigated with utmost care, honoring your limits. Compromise should ensure that the burdens and benefits are shared equitably, ensuring that it never comes at the expense of one's own needs and self-respect.

Can compromise neutralize all opposition? Yes, most of the time. So, try! Deal with the conflict in a friendly, fair, frank, and firm manner. However, when negotiation takes a turn for the worse or the opposition is determined to deflate, defeat, and destroy your dream, then it's best to part ways. You may even need to initiate it! Sometimes, the best compromise possible is making no deal at all. While this may not be an ideal outcome, it may be more beneficial to your organization than offering undue concessions to try and save face.

At its core, "compromise" embodies the spirit of cooperation and empathy. It's a tool for building bridges and fostering harmonious relationships. Yet, it is imperative to understand that compromise should never be a one-way street, where your own needs and wants are consistently sacrificed for others. This concept echoes the age-old adage, "*Give only what you can give without depleting yourself.*"

Respecting oneself is the cornerstone of healthy compromise. It's about recognizing your inherent worth and ensuring no one takes advantage of your willingness to find a middle ground. Like a firm handshake, self-respect establishes a boundary that communicates your limits and expectations clearly.

One of my friends, driven by a strong aspiration to succeed as a Star and in relentless pursuit of this dream, compromised her morals and values. In one of our heartfelt conversations, she became emotional and tearful. Regrettably, she entered into a relationship with her agent, who made promises to secure her the desired role. As a result, she achieved success in her career, but unfortunately, she contracted AIDS as well!

As Ayad Akhtar, a Pulitzer Prize-winning playwright, beautifully expresses, "*The secret of a happy life is respect. Respect for yourself and respect for others.*"

Still, the question remains: Can one cultivate such leadership?

Would you be capable of learning and becoming an exceptional leader? Honestly, it is challenging to provide a definite answer to this question. To be transparent, I have not yet encountered a proven method for developing exceptional leaders, nor do I possess a comprehensive understanding of their emotional journeys. People have made some educated assumptions about the unique mindset of unconventional leaders through various studies and research. Could these individuals be channeling their personal ambitions towards something different? Might they be suppressing their egos due to deep and complex reasons rooted in childhood experiences? It is difficult to determine. And, perhaps more significantly, do the psychological origins of unconventional leadership hold any greater significance than those of charisma or intelligence?

However, based on my personal experience and studies, it seems that certain individuals may struggle to prioritize the needs of a larger and more enduring cause over their own desires. For these individuals, their primary focus will always be on personal gain, such as fame, wealth, power, and recognition. Their work will never truly be about the positive impact they can make or the contributions they can offer. Ironically, the drive and ambition that often lead people to become traditional leaders conflict with the humility necessary to become exceptional leaders.

However, some individuals may have the potential to evolve—the capability may reside within them, perhaps buried, ignored, or simply nascent. Under the right circumstances—such as self-reflection, guidance from a mentor, supportive parents, or impactful life events- this potential can start to flourish. Some of the leaders I know had significant life experiences that might have sparked the development of the seed. This could be their near-death experience—recovering from a fatal illness or losing someone they loved. The great Ashoka, for example, was radically affected by his war experiences.

In summary, quantum leadership is a highly satisfying, honest, and influential concept that is likely essential for achieving greatness. However, providing a simple list of steps for quantum leadership would undermine the significance of the idea. Drawing from my own experience, my best suggestion is to engage in the other positive disciplines we have uncovered on the path to greatness. We have discovered a strong correlation between these disciplines and outstanding leadership, so consciously striving to lead using these practices can help you move in the right direction. While there is no guarantee that this will transform executives into entirely unconventional leaders, it does offer a tangible starting point, particularly for those who are driven to succeed.

Even those of us who have thoroughly researched and written this book are still trying to determine if we will reach the peak of quantum leadership. Nonetheless, we find great inspiration in the concept and the leaders we have studied. Whether or not we attain the highest level, it is worthwhile to strive for it, as it will undoubtedly enrich our own lives and positively impact everything we influence.

***

PART-III

Icons of Mythology

- **Management Interpolation**

In the ever-evolving landscape of leadership, it is crucial to explore unconventional avenues that can inspire and illuminate the path forward. One such uncharted territory is the realm of mythology, an ancient source of timeless wisdom that transcends generations. By intertwining myth and leadership, we open the door to a world of innovation and inspiration, where age-old tales breathe fresh life into modern challenges.

Harnessing the Wisdom of Indian Scriptures: Our Indian scriptures, be it the Arthashastra [xiv], Ramayana [xv], or Mahabharata[xvi], are veritable goldmines of management acumen. Within their verses lies a treasure trove of wisdom that transcends time and culture. These narratives, often regarded as sacred and spiritual, also serve as a wellspring of practical insights for modern management.

The Epic Mahabharata, for instance, stands as a prime example of the rich tapestry of management principles woven into myth. Its characters, dilemmas, and strategies provide a compelling analogy for modern leadership. Arjuna [xvii], Yudhishthira, and Krishna [xviii] represent archetypes of leadership, each offering a distinct lesson for managers. Arjuna's unwavering focus and determination, Yudhishthira's commitment to righteousness, and Krishna's astute counsel demonstrate the varied facets of

Leadership offers a diverse palette for managers to draw from.

Moreover, these stories are not confined to mere theoretical examples. They provide actionable insights, offering pragmatic solutions to the dilemmas faced by contemporary managers. As we embark on this mythological journey, we find that the Mahabharata, for instance, offers sapient guidance on decision-making, conflict resolution, and the art of strategic planning.

Teaching Workplace Values: Beyond the realm of strategic insight, mythology also serves as an excellent conduit for instilling crucial workplace values. Leadership, integrity, and ethical decision-making are not just buzzwords but pillars of a thriving and responsible organization. By using mythological narratives, these values can be imparted in an engaging and relatable manner.

Consider the Ramayana, where Lord Rama's unwavering commitment to dharma and ethics resonates deeply with contemporary leaders. His trials and tribulations offer a paragon of leadership based on ethical decision-making. The story of his unwavering commitment to truth, even at great personal cost, serves as an inspiring example for leaders navigating the complexities of a modern corporate world.

Greek Mythology and Business Relevance: While Indian mythology is a rich source of wisdom, Greek mythology too has an enduring relevance to modern business and management challenges. The pantheon of Greek gods and heroes is a repository of timeless narratives, each brimming with lessons that transcend the sands of time.

The tale of the legendary Greek king of Ithaca, Odysseus[xix], in Homer's "The Odyssey" offers insights into strategy, wisdom, adaptability, and resilience—crucial attributes for leaders in today's dynamic marketplace. Odysseus' journey home after battling in the Trojan War[xx], fraught with obstacles and setbacks, mirrors the unpredictable twists and turns that business leaders often encounter. By interpreting his story, managers can glean creative ways to overcome obstacles and steer their organizations toward their desired destinations.

Additionally, the myth of Sisyphus[xxi], who was condemned to push a boulder uphill for eternity, serves as a potent metaphor for perseverance and the never-ending struggles that leaders face. Sisyphus's relentless determination in the face of futility can inspire leaders to persist in their quests, even when the odds seem insurmountable.

I. Strategic Alliances and Teams

The Mahabharata, one of India's most celebrated epics, reveals a compelling narrative that transcends time and speaks directly to the essence of modern leadership. The allegory of King Dhritrashtra's[xxii] blindness and his advisor Sanjay presents an intriguing parable that not only emphasizes the significance of team building and alliances but also raises critical questions about the fine line between strategic blindness, biases, and personal responsibility.

In the Mahabharata, King Dhritrashtra serves as a poignant symbol of leadership that transcends physical limitations. Blind since birth, he ascends the throne, overseeing a kingdom on the brink of an epic war. However, he is unable to witness the unfolding events on the battlefield firsthand. In this challenging situation, Sanjay, his trusted charioteer and advisor, assumes a crucial role. Sanjay's duty was to provide a vivid account of the unfolding events, enabling Dhritrashtra to make informed decisions.

Dhritrashtra's reliance on Sanjay's insights carries profound relevance for modern leadership, reflecting the concept of 'strategic blindness.' In today's fast-paced and complex corporate world, leaders often find themselves in a situation akin to Dhritrashtra's, where they must depend on the expertise and insights of their advisors, teams, and alliances to craft strategies and make crucial decisions.

This practice embodies the essence of delegation and team building, where leaders leverage the collective knowledge and talents of their teams to navigate complex challenges. 'Strategic blindness' acknowledges that leaders cannot possess all knowledge and expertise themselves, just as Dhritrashtra's physical inability to witness the battlefield. However, it also presents a conundrum.

While the concept of 'strategic blindness' fosters collaboration and reliance on experts, it can inadvertently lead to a sense of detachment from the consequences of decisions. Dhritrashtra, relying on Sanjay's narration, could choose to distance himself from the stark realities of the battlefield. This brings us to a critical question for contemporary leaders: How much personal responsibility should they shoulder when making decisions?

The concept of 'strategic blindness' introduces a layer of ambiguity to the issue of accountability. Leaders who excessively rely on their advisors or introduce their own biases may find it easier to shift responsibility for the outcomes of their decisions. In extreme cases, this can lead to a sense of irresponsibility, potentially undermining the essence of effective leadership.

Finding the Balance: As we navigate this intricate landscape, the narrative of Dhritrashtra and Sanjay imparts an insightful lesson for modern leaders, underscoring the importance of striking a delicate balance between seeking expert guidance and embracing personal responsibility.

In essence, leaders should cherish 'strategic blindness' as a tool for informed decision-making, but also understand that the ultimate responsibility for the consequences of their decisions rests with them.

II. Learner's Curiosity

Leadership is a never-ending journey marked by an ongoing need for insight and growth. Even renowned figures like Rama, Krishna, and Arjuna recognized the importance of mentors in their personal and leadership growth. These stories highlight two essential qualities of effective leaders: an insatiable appetite for knowledge and a willingness to explore new information. When individuals seek to improve as leaders, many turn to mythology as a source of wisdom from the past. Rama, Krishna, and Arjuna—three legendary heroes—through the lenses of curiosity, education, and guidance. Despite their celestial status, these mythical heroes benefited from the counsel of wise elders during their growing or formative years. By exploring their experiences, we gain a valuable understanding of effective leadership and the significant role mentors play.

The function of a mentor extends beyond providing instruction; it is a collaborative process that encourages exploration, creates growth opportunities, and ignites the spark for future leadership.

Mentors as Catalysts for Change: Mentors offer more than simply information; they provide an additional lens through which leaders might experience the world. Mentors, like Krishna's advice to Arjuna on the battlefield, help leaders see things from different vantage points. This new viewpoint is essential for effective decision-making because it enables leaders to address problems with a comprehensive understanding of all their facets.

Furthermore, mentors offer constant encouragement and a strong sense of community. They are the rock upon which leaders can rest their shaky resolve in times of difficulty. A mentor's persistent mentoring can revitalize a leader's determination and feeling of purpose. A leader's self-awareness can be greatly improved through the crucible of mentoring. A leader's mentor has the unique capacity to highlight both the leader's strengths and areas for improvement. With this kind of insight, leaders may move forward with confidence and clarity, realizing their full potential. The ancient story of Arjuna's training under the guidance of gurus like Drona and Krishna provides a striking analogy to the transforming impact of mentoring. *Just as Krishna led Arjuna to victory on the battlefield, a mentor can provide a mentee with direction, support, and knowledge.*

III. The Prepared Mind

The Ramayana is also a valuable source of ancient wisdom, offering valuable lessons for us to learn from. By examining the experiences of the protagonists, Sita[xxiii] and Urmila, we can gain insights into leadership qualities. Their story highlights a fundamental truth: preparing for a situation is crucial for seizing the opportunity. Being always prepared, Sita accompanied her husband Rama[xxiv] into the forest, fully equipped to shield him from potential dangers. Her years of training as a skilled hunter and warrior, along with her deep knowledge of how to survive in the forest, gave her the strength and poise to handle the tasks.

This was very different from her sister Urmila, who was married to Laxman, the brother of Rama, and could have been a suitable choice for the same trip, but she wasn't as well-prepared as Sita. Delicate Urmila would not be able to survive the rigors of the forest because she didn't know how to get around in the bush. It was clear that she wasn't sturdy, and it might have been difficult for her to adapt to the forest's complex needs quickly. *Bamboo trees that remain underground for years demonstrate the importance of thorough planning ahead of time.* It stresses that readiness often grows slowly, making people stronger over time for tasks they didn't expect. Leaders who prioritize preparation, both in terms of their knowledge and their ability to adapt, can handle the challenges and uncertainties of their jobs with confidence and strength, much like Sita did when she had to protect Rama in the dark.

IV. Hardship Brings Greatness

Through suffering, character strength, and a commitment to justice, Rama set a leadership standard that will never be forgotten. It was hard for Rama to become great. He had to overcome obstacles. True leaders excel like this.

Everything was ready for Rama to rule Ayodhya. Happy moments and a long-held dream were fulfilled. Fate had other plans. Due to his difficult desert assignment, he had to give up his regal robes for austere clothing. The final test of his strength was this abrupt turn of circumstances. One instant will transform him from a prince to Lord Rama.

Rama's response to this unanticipated issue sets him apart. Without hesitation, he accepted the order with incomparable grace. His agreement to go into exile for fourteen years was based on his dedication to dharma, the righteous path. This gesture of absolute acceptance revealed his strength and prepared him for leadership.

In this challenging situation, Rama's leadership skills shone through. He proved that being excellent means tackling issues head-on and not giving up when things get tough. Rama was a model citizen because he always adhered to the law. His journey through the wilderness demonstrated his character, leadership, and devotion to dharma.

Instead of resting, Rama's absence made him a great leader. He persevered through wilderness hazards and asceticism to achieve his aim. These traits made him a superb leader, not just an heir to the throne.

The fact that Lord Rama's legacy endures is a testament to his enduring influence. Each leader must travel from the brink of kingship to the heart of the forest. Being great is a long, difficult road filled with challenges. Rama's narrative suggests that a leader's actual test is how they handle issues with honesty and resolution, rather than success.

Leadership is often confused with power and self-interest today. Rama's story teaches leadership through sacrifice and selflessness. True leaders, like Rama, view suffering as an opportunity for improvement. They demonstrate this by striving for justice and following dharma.

V. Dedication and Self-Belief

No matter how big or small, mythology is full of stories about people who, despite all odds, became famous because they were dedicated and believed in themselves. It's clear from the stories of Eklavya[xxv] and Karna[xxvi] that the human spirit has limitless potential and can reach incredible heights, even when it faces rejection and hardship.

Unlike many fortunate souls, Eklavya and Karna did not have teachers who guided them in acquiring information and skills. Their journey was marked by toughness, independence, and an unrelenting desire to improve. They didn't give up when they were turned down; instead, they embarked on a fantastic journey to learn and master new things, defying their circumstances.

Karna attempted to conceal his identity and origins so that he could learn from Parashurama, a renowned warrior-teacher. Karna did this brave thing because he was always hungry for knowledge and wanted to get better. His story demonstrates that the only way to be truly great is to remain committed to your goals, regardless of the obstacles that society or fate presents.

Eklavya, on the other hand, approached problems differently. Because he wasn't allowed to learn from Drona, who was the best shooting teacher, he made a clay figure of the person who turned him down. Because Eklavya was so dedicated, this copy of Drona became his teacher while he was away. He practiced with unmatched zeal every day, guided by his faith in himself and the replica's picture.

Both Karna and Eklavya have exhibited exceptional skills, surpassing even those of Arjuna. The tales of Eklavya and

Karna serve as a poignant reminder of the remarkable strength that can be found within oneself and the importance of persevering in the face of seemingly insurmountable challenges. Their unwavering commitment, their never-ending thirst for knowledge, and their refusal to let their conditions define them are truly inspiring. In their own unique ways, both Eklavya and Karna demonstrated the strong will of individuals who wouldn't let social norms, prejudice, or rejection deter them. They were experts in their fields because they were determined to learn and excel, even when the going was tough. They showed what ambition and commitment are all about by rising above their humble beginnings and leaving an indelible mark on history.

VI. Forgive and Forego

There are a handful of people in history who represent the concept of forgiveness and selflessness as profoundly as Lord Krishna. From infancy until death, his life was a tribute to the unselfish attitude that exemplifies the act of foregoing or giving up for the greater good. Lord Krishna's path is one of incredible sacrifice, an offering of his biological parents, birthplace, family, loves of life, a kingdom, and his entire body and soul to a higher goal.

Krishna's life was a never-ending story of unselfish love and infinite compassion. He was not constrained by human ambitions or ego; instead, his life was a living example of infinite love and generosity extended to everybody. He was the personification of truth and justice, a pillar of unshakeable integrity in a world rife with deception. Krishna never wavered from his objective, which was anchored in the well-being of humanity.

Krishna's influence as the most incredible God is enormous, and his teachings remain an eternal source of inspiration for us all. He was not only a divinity but also a profound guide on how to live with a pure heart and a mind free from worldly illusions. He urged us to seek truth and justice even if it seemed uncomfortable or difficult. His message was straightforward but profound: the path to enlightenment and self-realization begins with forgiveness, compassion, and selflessness.

"*Your life will not end with death,*" said Zain Hashmi, a Pakistani activist. You are invincible. You were always present, and you will always be."

This idea resonates with the timeless essence of Krishna's teachings, which emphasize that forgiveness and selflessness are not limited to mortal existence but transcend time and place. Forgiveness and letting go are not just acts of charity, but also potent tools for personal transformation and spiritual growth. By liberating ourselves from responsibilities that sometimes weigh us down and distort our view, we can shed our ego and attachment. In this surrender, we realize the limitless stream of love and kindness that exists within ourselves, mirroring Lord Krishna's glorious characteristics.

VII. Humility and Modesty

Lord Krishna is a shining example of modesty, a living monument to the harmonious union of strength and tenderness. Despite his remarkable exploits, such as raising the enormous mountain Govardhan, Krishna was known by pejorative titles, including *Murli-Dhar* (Flute-Master), *Makan-Chor* (Butter Thief), and *Ranchhor* (Runaway from War). These nicknames were not an insult to his character but rather a reflection of his profound humility. Krishna's capacity to endure these titles with grace demonstrates his extraordinary humility. He was a living example of how to wield enormous power while remaining grounded in humility. He showed that true strength is defined not by arrogance or dominance but by a heart that understands the beauty of modesty.

Krishna's compassion was limitless. When God Indra's anger threatened the people of Gokul, he selflessly protected them by raising the massive Govardhan mountain as a shield, shielding them from the impending deluge. His actions demonstrated a profound empathy for others' suffering and an unwavering commitment to their well-being.

Krishna's bravery was reflected in his valiant struggles against Kamsa's[xxvii] demonic forces. He faced evil with bravery that mirrored his inner strength, demonstrating that bravery and modesty are not mutually exclusive characteristics. His steadfast dedication to preserving the values of dharma was demonstrated by his firm stance against injustice.

His life was a never-ending pursuit of the highest principles, a goal to serve humanity selflessly and modestly. Even if his actions were supernatural, he stayed grounded in the domain of humanity, reminding us that true grandeur is inextricably linked to humility.

A timeless and cross-cultural truth is revealed in these epics, and it demonstrates that genuine leaders are shaped, rather than born, by adversity. Some examples of these legendary figures demonstrate that everyone, regardless of their past or current circumstances, can aspire to become a leader. By drawing on our own reserves of fortitude and resiliency, we demonstrate that learning from one's mistakes and persevering in the face of setbacks are necessary for truly extraordinary accomplishments.

Let us focus on internal growth and steadfast commitment to a greater cause rather than seeking external praise. I'm sure you are all familiar with the ancient tale "Vikram and Betaal," which is based on a collection of Sanskrit stories known as Betaal-pachisi—an enchanting collection of twenty-five stories about ghosts penned by the 11th-century Kashmiri poet Somdev Bhatt.

Just to recap, *the tales mention a sorcerer who asks King Vikramaditya to fetch a ghost from a crematorium. The only way to fetch a ghost is to keep one's mouth shut while transporting the ghost back. But the ghost is very clever and determined to escape; he tells the king a story and asks a question at the end. "Answer the question, Vikramaditya!" he challenges the king. "If you keep your mouth shut despite knowing the answer, your head will burst into a thousand pieces. You are not fit to be a king if you don't know the answer. I'm sure the sorcerer will use me to destroy you."*

As leaders, we strive to emulate Vikramaditya by solving problems, unravelling puzzles, and proving our worth. A leader, whether a king or a CEO, is a problem solver who can make crucial decisions in challenging situations.

No one else is supposed to provide answers or advice. In a way, they are like the unrelated ghost Betaal, who hangs upside down and offers a topsy-turvy view of all things. Leaders gain insights by questioning everything and acquiring knowledge rather than receiving it. Therefore, leaders must seek out challenges, even in unproductive spaces like crematoriums, to find the ghost. The choice of a crematorium is deliberate, as it does not generate revenue. However, if the Betaal in the crematorium can inspire individuals to become exceptional leaders like Vikramaditya, then those who return to the organization or kingdom from this experience will possess the ability to make exceptional decisions that generate revenue and mitigate losses under challenging environments.

***

End Notes

---

[i] **Herbert Spencer** (April 1820–December 1903) was an English polymath active as a philosopher, psychologist, biologist, sociologist, and anthropologist. Spencer originated the expression "survival of the fittest," which he coined in Principles of Biology (1864) after reading Charles Darwin's 1859 book On the Origin of Species. The term strongly suggests natural selection; however, Spencer saw evolution as extending into realms of sociology and ethics, and thus also supported Lamarckism. Spencer developed an all-encompassing conception of evolution as the progressive development of the physical world, biological organisms, the human mind, and human culture and societies.

[ii] **Gordon Willard Allport** (1897–1967) was an American psychologist. Allport was one of the first psychologists to focus on the study of personality and is often referred to as one of the founding figures of personality psychology. He contributed to the development of value scales and rejected both a psychoanalytic approach to personality, which he thought was often too deeply interpretive, and a behavioral approach, which he believed did not provide sufficiently in-depth interpretations from its data. Instead of these popular approaches, he developed an eclectic **theory based on traits.** He emphasized the uniqueness of each individual and the importance of the present context, as opposed to history, for understanding the personality.

[iii] **Blake and Mouton**, in their managerial grid model, proposed five leadership styles based on two axes - concern for the task versus concern for people. They suggested that the ideal is the "team style", which balances concern for the task with concern for people. Scouller (2011) argued that this ideal approach may not be suitable in all circumstances, such as emergencies or turnarounds.

[iv] **Fred Edward Fiedler** (1922–2017) was one of the leading researchers in industrial and organizational psychology in the 20th century. He was born in Vienna, Austria, and immigrated to the United States in 1938. Fiedler studied psychology at the University of Chicago and later joined the University of Illinois, where he became the director of the Group

Effectiveness Laboratory. He also held positions at the University of Washington, where he directed organizational research until his retirement in 1992. Fiedler's contributions to the field include shifting the focus from traits to leadership styles and behaviors and introducing the Fiedler Contingency Model in 1967.

[v] **Contingency theory** is an organizational theory that claims that there is no best way to organize a corporation, to lead a company, or to make decisions. Instead, the optimal course of action is contingent (dependent) upon the internal and external situation. Contingent leaders are flexible in choosing and adapting to suitable strategies for change in a particular situation at a given point in time, thereby guiding the organization's operations.

[vi] **The Situational Leadership Theory** was developed by Dr Paul Hersey and Dr Ken Blanchard while they were working on the textbook Management of Organizational Behavior. Originally known as the Life Cycle Theory of Leadership. The Situational Leadership Theory is part of a group of leadership theories developed at Ohio State University in the 1960s. These theories suggest that a combination of task behavior and relationship behavior determines leadership styles. Different terms are used to describe these behaviors, such as initiating structure or direction for task behavior and consideration or socioemotional support for relationship behavior. Other similar leadership models include Blake and Mouton's Managerial Grid and Reddin's 3D Theory. In the late 1970s and early 1980s, Hersey and Blanchard developed their own versions of the Situational Leadership Theory. In 2018, it was decided that the Blanchard version would be trademarked as SLII, and the Hersey version would remain as Situational Leadership.

The primary concept of the Situational Leadership Model is that there is no single best leadership style. Effective leadership is based on adapting to the readiness level of the individuals or groups being led. It also depends on the task that needs to be accomplished. The model focuses on leadership style and the maturity level of the individuals or groups.

[vii] **John Eric Adair** (born 18 May 1934) is a British academic who is a leadership theorist and author of more than forty books (translated into eighteen languages) on business, military, and other leadership.

[viii] **James MacGregor Burns** (1918–2014) was an American historian and political scientist, presidential biographer, and authority on leadership

studies. He was the Woodrow Wilson Professor of Government Emeritus at Williams College and Distinguished Leadership Scholar at the James MacGregor Burns Academy of Leadership of the School of Public Policy at the University of Maryland, College Park. In 1971, Burns received the Pulitzer Prize and the National Book Award in History and Biography for his work on America's 32nd president, Roosevelt: The Soldier of Freedom. Burns shifted the focus of leadership studies from the traits and actions of great men to the interaction of leaders and their constituencies as collaborators working towards mutual benefit. He was best known for his contributions to the transactional, transformational, aspirational, and visionary schools of leadership theory.

[ix] **Transformational leadership** is a theory of leadership where a leader works with teams or followers beyond their immediate self-interests to identify needed change, creating a vision to guide the change through influence and inspiration, and executes the change in tandem with committed members of a group. This change in self-interest elevates the follower's levels of maturity and ideals, as well as their concerns for achievement.

Transformational leadership inspires people to achieve unexpected or remarkable results. It gives workers autonomy over specific jobs as well as the authority to make decisions once they have been trained. This induces a positive change in the followers' attitudes and the organization as a whole. Transformational leaders typically perform four distinct behaviors, also known as the four Is. These behaviors are inspirational motivation, idealized influence, intellectual stimulation, and individualized consideration.

[x] **Charismatic authority** is a concept of leadership developed by the German sociologist Max Weber. It involves a type of organization or a type of leadership in which authority derives from the charisma of the leader. This stands in contrast to two other types of authority: legal authority and traditional authority. Each of the three types forms part of Max Weber's tripartite classification of authority.

[xi] **Servant leadership** is a leadership philosophy in which the goal of the leader is to serve. This differs from traditional leadership, where the leader's primary focus is the success and growth of their company or organization. A servant leader shares power, prioritizes the needs of employees, and helps people develop and perform at their best.

[xii] **Robert Kiefner Greenleaf** (1904–1990) was the founder of the modern servant leadership movement and the Greenleaf Center for Servant Leadership. Greenleaf was born in Terre Haute, Indiana, in 1904. After graduating from Carleton College in Minnesota, he began working for AT&T, then known as the American Telephone and Telegraph Company. For the next 40 years, he researched management, development, and education. He became suspicious that the power-centered authoritarian leadership style prevalent in U.S. institutions was not working, so in 1964, he took early retirement to found the Greenleaf Center for Servant Leadership (initially called the Center for Applied Ethics).

[xiii] The **Oxford Leadership Academy** (OLA) is an international leadership training consultancy with its headquarters in Oxford, United Kingdom. The firm specialises in leadership development, strategy execution, and culture change in complex global organisations. It has 900,000 alumni and 215 consultants and associates in 28 countries.

[xiv] **The Arthashastra** is an ancient Indian Sanskrit text that covers statecraft, political science, economics, and military strategy. It is traditionally attributed to Kautilya, also known as Vishnugupta and Chanakya, who was a scholar and advisor to Emperor Chandragupta Maurya. However, some scholars debate the authorship of the text. It was likely composed, expanded, and edited by multiple authors over several centuries between the 2nd century BCE and the 3rd century CE. Scholars rediscovered and published the Arthashastra in the early 20th century, after it had been lost for nearly 1,000 years since the 12th century. In recent years, there has been a renewed interest in the text, particularly among those trying to understand India's potential global power and its unique approach to defining power.

This Sanskrit text, known as Arthashastra, covers a wide range of topics including political science, economics, and statecraft. It discusses government, law, courts, ethics, economics, trade, diplomacy, war, peace, and the responsibilities of a king. The text also incorporates elements of Hindu philosophy and provides information on agriculture, mining, medicine, and wildlife conservation. It advises the king to take measures for social welfare during times of crisis, such as building irrigation systems and exempting taxes for those affected. Other Hindu texts, such as the Manusmriti, influenced the text.

[xv] **The Ramayana** (/rɑːˈmɑːjənə/; Sanskrit: रामायणम्) is a Sanskrit epic from ancient India, one of the two important epics of Hinduism known as the Itihasas (history), the other being the Mahābhārata. The epic, traditionally ascribed to the Maharishi Valmiki, narrates the life of Rama, a prince of Ayodhya in the kingdom of Kosala. The epic follows his fourteen-year exile to the forest urged by his father, King Dasharatha, on the request of Rama's stepmother Kaikeyi; his travels across forests in the Indian subcontinent with his wife Sita and brother Lakshmana; the kidnapping of Sita by Ravana, the king of Lanka, that resulted in war; and Rama's eventual return to Ayodhya, along with Sita, to be crowned king amidst jubilation and celebration.

Scholars believe the Ramayana text originated between the 7th and 4th centuries BCE, with additions made until the 3rd century CE. It is one of the largest ancient epics, comprising approximately 24,000 verses divided into seven chapters. The Ramayana belongs to the genre of Itihasa (history), which combines narratives of past events with teachings on the goals of human life. There are various versions of the Ramayana in different Indian languages, as well as adaptations in Buddhist and Jain traditions, and it has influenced the poetry, culture, and moral values of Hindu and Buddhist societies. The main characters of the Ramayana embody virtues that are considered essential for citizens and the functioning of a just society.

[xvi] **The Mahabharata** is an ancient Sanskrit epic poem from India. It is considered an important source of information on the development of Hinduism between 400 BCE and 200 CE. Hindus view it as a text about moral law and history. The poem, which was completed around 400 CE, tells the story of a struggle for power between two groups of cousins, the Kauravas and the Pandavas. It consists of almost 100,000 couplets, divided into 18 sections. Although the authorship of the poem is unclear, it is traditionally attributed to the sage Vyasa. The date and historical accuracy of the central war in the Mahabharata are subjects of debate.

[xvii] **Arjuna** (Sanskrit: अर्जुन), also known as **Partha** and **Dhananjaya**, is the central figure, a protagonist. Arjuna was the son of Kunti, the wife of Kuru King Pandu, and the god Indra, who fathered him as a result of Pandu's curse. In the Mahabharata, Arjuna is depicted as a skilled archer from an early age, as a student who earns the favor of his preceptor, Drona, as the primary adversary of the Kauravas, and as the betrothed

of Draupadi, who becomes the common wife of the Pandavas. Arjuna is twice exiled, first for breaking a pact with his brothers, and again with his brothers after his oldest brother is tricked into gambling away the throne. During his first exile, Arjuna married Ulupi, Chitrāngadā, and Subhadra. From his four wives, Arjuna had four sons, one from each wife —Shrutakarma, Iravan, Babhruvahana, and Abhimanyu. During his second exile, Arjuna gained many celestial weapons. Despite being a warrior, Arjuna also possessed skills in music and dance. At the end of the epic, the Pandavas, accompanied by Draupadi, retire to the Himalayas, where everyone, in time, passes away to arrive in Heaven.

xviii **Krishna** (/ˈkrɪʃnə/) is a principal deity in Hinduism. He is the god of protection, compassion, tenderness, and love, and is one of the most popular and widely revered among Hindu divinities. The anecdotes and narratives of Krishna's life are generally titled as *Krishna Līlā*. He is a central character in the *Mahabharata* and the Bhagavad Gita and is mentioned in many Hindu philosophical, theological, and mythological texts. They portray him in various perspectives: as a godchild, a prankster, a model lover, a divine hero, and the universal supreme being. His iconography reflects these legends, depicting him in various stages of his life, such as an infant eating butter, a young boy playing a flute, a young boy with Radha, or surrounded by female devotees, or a friendly charioteer giving counsel to Arjuna.

xix In Greek and Roman mythology, **Odysseus** (/əˈdɪsiəs/ *ə-DISS-ee-əs*]), is a legendary Greek king of Ithaca and the hero of Homer's epic poem, The *Odyssey*. Odysseus also plays a key role in Homer's *Iliad* and other works in that same epic cycle.

Son of Laërtes and Anticlea, husband of Penelope, and father of Telemachus, Acusilaus, and Telegonus. Odysseus is renowned for his intellectual brilliance, guile, and versatility *(polytropos)* and is thus known by the epithet Odysseus the Cunning (Greek: μῆτις, translit. *mêtis*, lit. "Cunning intelligence"). He is most famous for his *nostos*, or "homecoming," which took him ten eventful years after the decade-long Trojan War.

xx **Trojan War:** After Paris of Troy took Helen from her husband, Menelaus, king of Sparta, the Achaeans (Greeks) waged the Trojan War against Troy. In Greek mythology, the war has been narrated in many works of literature, notably Homer's Iliad. During the tenth year of the decade-long siege of Troy, the Iliad describes four days and two nights; meanwhile, the Odyssey recounts Odysseus' journey home. Roman poets, such as Virgil and Ovid, drew inspiration from episodes of the war, similar to those found in Greek tragedy. The ancient Greeks believed that Troy was located near the Dardanelles and that the Trojan War was a historical event that occurred in the 13th or 12th century BC. The war and the city were widely considered nonhistorical by the mid-19th century AD, but in 1868, the German archaeologist Heinrich Schliemann met Frank Calvert, who convinced Schliemann that Troy was in Hisarlik. According to Schliemann and others, this claim is now accepted.

xxi In Greek mythology, **Sisyphus** or **Sisyphos** (/ˈsɪsɪfəs/; Ancient Greek: Σίσυφος *Sísyphos*) was the founder and king of Ephyra (now known as Corinth). He was a devious tyrant who killed visitors to show off his power. This violation of the sacred hospitality tradition greatly angered the gods. They punished him for the trickery of others, including his cheating death twice. The gods forced him to roll an immense boulder up a hill, only for it to roll back down every time it neared the top, repeating this action for eternity. Through the classical influence on modern culture, tasks that are both laborious and futile are therefore described as **Sisyphean** (/sɪsɪˈfiːən/).

xxii **Dhritarashtra** (Sanskrit: धृतराष्ट्र) was a Kuru king and the father of the Kauravas in the Hindu epic Mahabharata. He was the King of the Kuru Kingdom, with its capital at Hastinapur. He was born to Vichitravirya's first wife, Ambika. Dhritarashtra was born blind. He fathered one hundred sons and one daughter, Dushala, by his wife, Gandhari, and a son, Yuyutsu, by his wife's maid. These children, including the eldest son, Duryodhana, but excluding Yuyutsu and Dushala, came to be known as the Kauravas.

xxiii **Sita** (Sanskrit: सीता), also known as Siya, Janaki, Maithili, Vaidehi, and Bhumija, is a Hindu goddess and the female protagonist of the Hindu epic *Ramayana*. She is traditionally known for her dedication, self-sacrifice, courage, and purity. Described as the daughter of Bhūmi (the earth), Sita was raised as the adopted daughter of King Janaka of Videha. In her youth, she chose Rama, the prince of Ayodhya, as her husband in a swayamvara (marriage). After the swayamvara, she accompanied her husband to his kingdom, but later chose to accompany her husband, along with her brother-in-law Lakshmana, into exile. While in exile, the trio settled in the Dandaka forest, where Ravana, the Rakshasa king of Lanka, abducted her. She was imprisoned in the garden of Ashoka Vatika in Lanka until Rama, who slayed her captor, rescued her. In some versions of the epic, Rama asks Sita to undergo Agni Pariksha (a fire ordeal) before accepting her as his wife. After proving her purity, Rama and Sita return to Ayodhya, and the people crown them as king and queen. One day, a man questions Sita's fidelity. To prove her innocence and maintain his own and the kingdom's dignity, Rama sends Sita into the forest near Valmiki's ashram. Years later, Sita returns to the womb of her mother, the Earth, to be released from a cruel world and as a testament to her purity after she reunites with her two sons, Kusha and Lava, and their father, Rama.

[xxiv] **Rama** (/ˈrɑːmə/) is a principal deity in Hinduism. Rama was born to Kaushalya and Dasharatha in Ayodhya, the capital of the Kingdom of Kosala. His siblings included Lakshmana, Bharata, and Shatrughna. He married Sita. Although born into a royal family, Rama's life is described in Hindu texts as one marked by unexpected changes, including exile into impoverished and difficult circumstances, as well as challenges posed by ethical questions and moral dilemmas. Of all his travails, the most notable is the kidnapping of Sita by demon-king Ravana, followed by the determined and epic efforts of Rama and Lakshmana to gain her freedom and destroy the evil Ravana against great odds. The entire life story of Rama, Sita, and their companions allegorically discusses the duties, rights, and social responsibilities of an individual. It illustrates dharma and dharmic living through model characters.

[xxv] **Ekalavya** (Sanskrit: एकलव्य) is a character from the Indian epic Mahabharata. His parents abandoned him as an infant, and Hiranyadhanus, the Nishada chief, adopted him. Hiranyadhanus was a powerful commander under King Jarasandha. Ekalavya, inspired by witnessing Drona teach archery to the royal princes, approached him and asked to become his student. However, the Kuru princes mocked him for his low birth. He then collected the mud on which Drona walked and created a statue of him in the forest. He dedicated himself to self-study and practiced archery in front of the statue every day. One day, Drona and his students venture into the forest with a dog from the Kurus. The dog starts barking but suddenly stops, and they find arrows in its mouth. Drona is amazed and worried because he promised to make

Arjuna the finest archer. They see Ekalavya with his bow, and Drona asks him where he learned archery. Ekalavya says he learned it from Drona and shows him a statue to prove it. Arjuna was angry and reminded Drona of his promise. Drona decides that Ekalavya must give him a gift as payment. Ekalavya offers to do anything, and Drona asks him to cut off his thumb. Ekalavya happily does so and gives it to Drona.

xxvi **Karna**, also known as **Vasusena**, **Anga-raja**, and **Radheya,** is one of the main protagonists of the Hindu epic *Mahābhārata*. He is the son of the sun god Surya and Princess Kunti (mother of the Pandavas), and thus a demigod of royal birth. Kunti was granted the boon to bear a child with desired divine qualities by the gods. Without much knowledge, Kunti invoked the sun god to confirm if it was indeed true. Karna was secretly born to an unmarried Kunti in her teenage years, and fearing outrage and backlash from society over her premarital pregnancy, Kunti had no choice but to abandon the newly born Karna adrift in a basket on the Ganges in the hope of foster parents. When Karna was discovered, his foster parents, Radha and Adhiratha Nandana, who worked as charioteers for King Dhritarashtra, adopted and raised him. Karna grew up to be an accomplished warrior of extraordinary abilities, a gifted speaker, and a loyal friend of Duryodhana. He was appointed king of Anga (present-day Bihar and Bengal) by Duryodhana. Karna joined Duryodhana's side in the Kurukshetra War. He was a key warrior who aimed to kill the third Pandava, Arjuna, but died in battle with him during the war. He is a tragic hero in the *Mahabharata*, like Aristotle's literary category of "flawed righteous man." He meets his biological mother late in the epic and discovers that he is the older half-brother of those he is fighting against. Symbolically, Karna represents someone who, given his circumstances, should have been loved but wasn't. However, he becomes a man of exceptional abilities willing to give his love and life as a loyal friend. As his character develops in the epic, major emotional and dharma dilemmas (duty, ethics, and morals) are raised and discussed.

xxvii **Kamsa** (Sanskrit: कंस) was the tyrant ruler of the Vrishni kingdom, with its capital at Mathura. He is variously described in Hindu literature as either a human or an asura; The Puranas describe him as an asura, while the Harivamśa describes him as an asura reborn in the body of a man. He was the cousin of Devaki, the mother of the deity Krishna; Krishna ultimately fulfilled a prophecy by slaying Kamsa.

Other Books by the Author